Secret Diary of a Camp Counselor

By Lucy Harper

Published in the United Kingdom by:

Bursea Books

www.burseabooks.com

ISBN: 978-0-9571552-1-3

This book is a work of non-fiction based on the life, experiences and recollections of the author from the summer of 2005. The names of some people, places, dates and sequences have been changed to protect the privacy of others.

www.secretdiaryofacampcounselor.com

Follow me on Twitter @USCampCounselor and
like 'Secret Diary of a Camp Counselor' on Facebook

Thank you Waiels, Mel, Lisa, Jules, Fiona, Michelle and Chloe for helping me. I'm lucky to know you all x

Contents

"To my best friend Lucy H,

This is a present for you to take to Camp Rockbear in Winkworth, New York, in ruddy America!

Use it to write your feelings in when you feel down, and just think of me. Make sure you record all the fun stuff too – I can't wait to read it when you get back!

Have a great time and I'll miss you.

Woot!

Love you loads, love Hannah <3"

Session One

Sunday 5th June

11.15am Heathrow Airport can be pretty lonely when you're by yourself. I haven't met anyone from Camp Rockbear yet, so I'm just sat on my own. I hope I'm put next to someone from my camp on the plane, I should've asked that at the orientation in Manchester. Nothing very interesting has happened so far – mum and dad left me, bit sad to say bye. I'll write when I have a friend, hopefully soon.

11:42am I'm really nervous. I'm too scared to approach anyone – wish I'd arranged to meet someone through those emails I sent a few months ago. I keep seeing people my age by themselves wandering around, they must be for camp, but I'm too scared to ask. Eugh, I hate being such a weed. I've wanted to come to camp for ages and now that I'm on my way, I'm terrified. I remember telling mum I'd applied last December.
Mum: "Why?"

It just looked so much fun and I wanted to work abroad for the summer – camp seemed like the cheapest thing to do. Last year all my friends from home and me just got jobs in the local town during the summer holidays, she thought I'd just do that again. But I went to the recruitment fair in January and got chatting to the camp director. He offered me a job as a DJ and that was that. I'm *so* excited to be in America for the summer and getting to just listen to music and play on the decks all day. Rockbear is one of the biggest camps in New York, actually in America I think. It's also one of the most expensive – at about $1000+ a week, wow.

12:09pm It feels like the first day of university again. I don't like making friends when you *have* to make friends. I'm alright chatting to people when it's not expected, like in clubs and bars or just in random situations, but when I have to be friends with someone I find it difficult to know what to say. And I'm shit at approaching them. I really don't want to be like this. I don't know what I think will happen – they're not going to be horrible are they? No one ever has been. I'm rambling. I'm trying to look busy writing so no one comes up to me. God I'm pathetic. I have nothing to write, but I'm writing because I'm too scared someone will catch my eye and talk to me, even though I want them to. The nerves have sent me crazy.

12:32pm Ok, I've moved to the departures lounge and here are all the people I saw wandering around on their own. I can see all the yellow CCUSA luggage tags on their bags now, so they're definitely going to camp and New York for the overnight orientation at Columbia University. I think it's just to fill us in a bit more about camp life before we get the bus to our camps. I've still got loads of questions.

I wonder which one Emily is? She was one of the few that replied to the email I sent out to the Rockbear email address list we were given. She didn't seem too keen on making friends beforehand though, so I didn't bother emailing back. I was trying to be cool, dammit.

12:45pm Everyone looks scared. I think I'll just carry on writing, I'm too anxious to look up. It's actually pretty funny really. I bet everyone here said, 'meeting new people' was one of their main reasons for coming to camp, but no one is actually talking to each other. Just realised we have got designated seats on our tickets, so I'm hoping they've put people from the same camps together. Argh, they've just announced the flight is going to be delayed. Really got nothing to write, I'm nervously rambling again. Right, I'm going to put my pen away, grow some balls and look up. Here goes...

1:48pm On the plane now and I still haven't spoken to anyone. I saw a few people chat to each other here and there. I'm thinking it was to ask which camp they were going to, and then when they found it wasn't the same one, they just didn't bother talking anymore. This is obviously me making up paranoid stories in my head. I'm sat on the end of the row next to some old people – pretty sure they're not going to Rockbear. There are some girls my age who I noticed had CCUSA luggage tags on their bags in front of me all talking to each other, I wish I was sat with them. I bet I would talk if I was with them. Argh, I'll just watch a film instead.

2.07pm Hmmm, got my earphones in, but not on. Just heard them say Camp Rockbear. They're all going to make friends without me. How can I join in? Right, big moment...

2:32pm Yay, spoke to them! The girl in front of me is one of the girls I'd emailed before, she's doing circus trapeze at the camp, sounds pretty cool. I told her I was the DJ – I always feel a bit of an idiot when I say that – she thought that was cool too though. It was difficult to talk because I had to sit up and talk over the top of the seat with the oldies next to me giving me dirty looks. I found out the girl sat next to her was Emily though. Ah, so happy I've chatted a bit to them – I won't feel so lonely and paranoid when we get to camp now. Relief!

11:16pm I'm in New York! On the bus from JFK airport to Columbia University I managed to make some more friends. They're from all over the world: Scotland, Australia, Manchester, Birmingham, Isle of Man, Dublin, Sheffield. Ok, maybe not the *world,* but still exciting.

Emily's working on the climbing wall and is actually from Brisbane in Australia, but she's studying Town Planning at Sheffield University and lives just up the road from me. I asked her if Australia was really like *Neighbours*. Haha, the only bit of Australian culture I know, along with *Home and Away* of course.

Emily: "No."

Hope she doesn't think I'm a twat – I really need to think before I speak.

When we got to Columbia University there was a woman there from CCUSA to welcome us. She gave us all a CCUSA-emblazoned green t-shirt each and said we needed to get in groups of sixes to share one of the student flats for the night. I managed to shimmy myself over to stand next to Emily and the other girls off the plane, so we went together up to flat 108. The flat has three rooms, each with two single beds, and we share the kitchen area, bathroom and lounge. We were meant to pair up and share a room, but there were only five of us so I volunteered to go by myself. Why did I do this? It would have been the perfect opportunity to make a friend. People scare me; I'm going to be rubbish at camp. I really don't know why I signed up for this. I bet I'm just going to spend the whole summer in my bunk with no friends.

We just watched a bit of *Family Guy* and then went to bed. Now I'm in my two-bed room sat by myself listening to the girls in the next room talking and laughing.

Monday 6th June

3:16pm I woke up to go to the toilet at about 5.30am and couldn't get back to sleep – think it's a mixture of jetlag and excitement. The flat was silent so I went for a mooch down Amsterdam Avenue, in New York! I felt a bit naughty being out from the university, especially as no one knew where I was, but it was a beautiful sunny morning and I wanted to see a bit of New York before we leave for camp. I walked along a few metres and found a run of bars and cafes. I would've loved to go out last night, but I was completely exhausted and *obviously* I would've been too scared to ask anyone.

By the time I got back it was breakfast in the main hall. Before I even got through the doors I could smell the fat of a fry-up. I really don't want to put on weight at camp so I just had cereal. I'm hoping camp will be a detox. We've been warned to expect a summer off alcohol, and that once you're at camp you're pretty much stuck with the food they give you. I hope it's healthy – surely it will be with all the fat kids everyone keeps going on about in America? The hall was filled with hundreds of counselors sat around the tables all in their CCUSA-issue t-shirts – it was a sea of green. Some tables were chatting away while others sat in awkward silence. I spotted Emily and perched myself on her chatty table.

After breakfast we had to queue up outside a room in the university to get a social security number to work in America. We sat waiting for *hours*. At least I made better friends with another one of the girls going to Rockbear in the queue though. Danielle and me got on pretty much instantly. She's from Birmingham – the nearest city to the village I'm from. She's pretty funny and has been to camp a few times before, not Camp Rockbear though. She said how she worked at an all girls' camp last year, which was fun, but they spent too much time singing around campfires and playing team-building games with bits of wood for her liking. She'd heard Rockbear was a bit crazier so she applied directly and got a job on the climbing wall. Hmmm, wonder what 'crazy' means? Excited!

Once everyone got their numbers we boarded the bus to Camp Rockbear. As I was getting on, the girl climbing the stairs in front of me was wearing white ¾ length tracksuit bottoms with 'Love Me' written in pink across the bum. Random, and hideous.

I'm sitting next to the Scottish girl I met on the plane; she's not talking much though. I reckon there must be about 100 people on here, all for Rockbear. I'm so nervous! I can't wait to see what the camp looks like. We've been on the bus for about three hours; surely it can't be much further? The camp is in New York, but upstate, in the mountains. I never even knew New York had mountains.

10.05pm I'm in a bunk with foreigners. No one's English, but I guess that's cool, in a way. One of my reasons to come here was to learn more about the world. I was just really hoping I'd be with one of the girls from the plane.

When we arrived we met the camp director Bud, who told us we'd all been assigned to a bunk. Bud was the guy who hired me originally at the camp director's fair in England. We'd got on instantly and it was good to see him again. I liked that he'd kind of taken a chance on me, as I didn't really have any of the skills they needed at camp. He said he hires on personality as much as skill though, so I could come along and DJ and do the camp radio.

There will be two to three other counselors in each bunk and up to 13 children. I'm in F13B, which means I'll be looking after 13-14 year olds. Bud gave us all a camp counselor handbook with a map in and I went on a solo mission to find F13B. I'm so shit at map reading, I ended up doing a lap of camp before I realised I was holding it upside down. My bunk was back where we got off the bus. Felt like a bit of an idiot struggling with my massive bag around camp only to end where I started, but at least I got to have a look around and get my bearings. The valley is surrounded by mountains and the air is so clean and fresh, it's lush.

On my tour I followed the curved path from the car park unintentionally downhill to the lake. I passed loads of bunks, still struggling with my suitcase behind me. It was a good few minutes' walk from where we were dropped off, but I could see the water sparkling in the distance and wanted to get closer.

The waterfront is amazing. There's a speedboat, canoes, water bikes, a big inflatable yellow trampoline and a huge white iceberg-shaped thing with handles and grips to climb up. From the beach there's a walkway pier reaching out about 20 metres and winding round to make a rectangular pool that I assume they use for swimming lessons. It has those lane dividers in it anyway. There was a row of lifejackets laid out on the beach, and an old woman was crouched counting them all. She must've sensed me there and looked at me like 'what-do-you-want', so I left. It's not about making enemies already.

Walking away from the waterfront I carried on where I'd left off and followed the path past what must have been the music studio – it had 'Pecs, Hugs and Rock n Roll' scrawled above the doorway anyway – I went by a door labelled 'costume' and up to a huge shed structure with a 'Visual Arts' sign covering the side. There was a big green space where the path curved around with a basketball court and a net for volleyball. I'd gone off on a bit of a tangent so I came back to the path, which led past the front offices near the car park. I saw the camp director, Bud, again and he was stood with some guy who I soon found out was the counselor who'd taught radio last year. He'd decided to come back at the last minute, so we needed to talk about how it was going to work out.

Old radio guy: "Errrm, there's not really enough space for two to teach radio. We can make it work, but errr, I didn't know they'd got someone else. I didn't know you were coming."

He seemed so sorry and inoffensive – I felt like I'd made the mistake, not Bud.

Me: "So, errr, what does that mean? Do I go home?"

Bud: "No, no, you're here now! Meet me tomorrow and we'll find you a job, don't worry."

He walked off, patting me on the head in a friendly, yet slightly patronising way as he passed.

It's a bit annoying, especially as I was really excited to be teaching radio and working with music all day out in the fresh air. I've told everyone at home I'm going to be a DJ and now I'm not. My school friends even made me a t-shirt saying 'DJ Harper' and gave me some CDs to play. Sad.

This was when I realised I'd gone the wrong way and needed to be back at the bunks I'd walked past at first. I said bye to the other radio guy and carried on along the main path to come back to where I started. The camp is huge! And absolutely amazing. It's probably about half a mile long – what I saw of it anyway.

I found my bunk near the dining hall in front of the car park; it's pretty big. From the outside the bunks are like the American wooden country houses you see on films. These ones are painted cream with the accents – windowsills, terrace, steps and skirting – in brown. There are two doors; one at the side up three steps which leads into the centre of the bunk, and one round the front leading up to the terrace that we share with the adjoining bunk. F13B is in the girls-only section. I bet they put our age group there to stop any midnight wanderers having access to the boys section. There's a grassy area out the front in the middle with seven bunks surrounding it in a circle and a thick row of trees separating the boys-only and the mixed section from us. Looks like they knew what they were doing when they designed this camp 30 years ago.

There's no electricity in the bunk, apparently we'll have some by the end of the week, *four* days away. It's freezing and the New York wilderness is so dark at night without any streetlights, house lights or car headlights passing.

Inside, the bunks have eight bunk beds lining three of the walls, rather than sticking out military style, with drawers underneath for clothes. The fourth wall has a big row of cubbyholes from floor to ceiling for more clothes. There's quite a bit of space to move around in here, probably not when the kids get here though, judging by all the scuffs and marks on the brown interior walls. There are curtainless windows along two of the facing sidewalls at a height where anyone who selects a bottom bunk will have the sun shining in on them in the morning. Some have shutters, but they don't look like they're attached very well. I'm going for a bed on the top; I reckon I'll get a better sleep up there. The bunks are pretty minging – I bet we're expected to clean them up – and the bathrooms are absolutely disgusting. I'm dreading doing a poo, everyone will be able to hear the plop.

My new bunk buddies are from America and South Africa. On first impressions they don't seem like much fun at all. The American girl looks like stereotypical trailer trash – complete with a cap, a slogan t-shirt, a bumbag, a few extra American pounds and a southern drawl. I'm sure she's lovely, but I don't think there are many lights on upstairs. After an awkward introduction she left. I chatted to the South African girl, she came to camp last year and I tagged along as she went to find her old friends. She introduced me, but I felt like a gooseberry with all their 'remember last year' talk, so I left them to it to find Emily.

Whenever you meet someone they want to know where you're from and what you're doing at university. I'm not really sure how much you can get from a person from this, but it seems to be standard.

Me: "Lucy Harper. Sheffield University. Communication Studies. From a little village near Birmingham in England, no you won't have heard of it."

I guess it's just making conversation, but it must be annoying for anyone who doesn't go to university, like the girl I met in the queue at Columbia, Danielle.

I really need to stop shaking people's hands so harshly when I meet them; I'm embarrassing myself.

Right, sleep time. I'm exhausted. My action plan to make friends tomorrow:

Sit with randoms at breakfast.

Make friends with the two other counselors in my bunk – it's going to be a long summer otherwise

Tuesday 7th June

8:16am Last night was odd. It was absolutely freezing in the bunk for starters. All I had for warmth in bed was the two bed sheets I got from the front office yesterday; I really need to get a sleeping bag when we have a day off. There are just the three of us in the bunk and we've all chosen beds that are spaced out so there wasn't any shared body warmth either. The doors and windows were rattling in the wind all night and the shutters kept slamming back against the frames. I've stupidly chosen the bed next to the door and the toilets, so I could hear the cold wind rattling through the bathroom all night. I don't think I slept at all.

I felt so vulnerable too – anyone could easily get in here, and I don't know any of these people. Sure, everyone has a CRB check to work here, but that doesn't necessarily mean anything. My bunk buddies could be crazy psychos for all I know – I wouldn't put it past the American one. There's no lock on the door either. I tried to imagine the sound I grew up with of dad locking the front door, having a bit of a cough and then climbing the stairs, to try and make me feel more secure, but it didn't work. Every time I managed to get the picture in my mind the door would open and slap against the frame again. I can't imagine ever getting a good night's sleep here; maybe I'm just being paranoid.

The bunk stinks as well. All the wood is damp from the storms they've been having, and it's obvious from the cobwebs that it hasn't been used since last summer. Our terrace light has smashed so it's pitch black – you can't even see your hand in front of your face. I needed the toilet in the night, but I was too scared to get down off my top bunk in case I made too much noise and annoyed the other girls.

I'm feeling pretty nervous about today, but I'm going to give having a good time my best shot. We've got five days until the kids come to set up the camp and get to know each other. I just hope I meet some fun people.

12:13pm After breakfast in the dining hall, which is just a three-minute walk from my bunk, we had a big staff meeting in the Kennedy Theatre. This is also really close to my bunk, just a few metres in front of the side door. It's a huge theatre in the round and the seats go way back high – not entirely sure how safe it is. I sat in between Danielle and Emily – I love how we just made instant friends. When I think about how scared I was in the airport I feel really proud of myself that I've got a little crew already.

Earl, who owns the camp, was there and Bud, the camp director. They actually look quite similar – both portly grey-haired men around 50-60ish in matching Camp Rockbear t-shirts and chinos. I wonder if they're related? They told us what they expect from us at camp and the basic rules:

– No relationships in front of the kids.

– No drinking on camp.

– No smoking ever, and if you get caught with a cigarette, no matter where you are, you're fired.

– Children come first, whatever happens.

– No swearing.

– Be friendly with the kids and hug them, but never touch them where a swimming costume does.

– Try not to be left alone with a kid.

There are four sessions per summer with 3-400 kids per session. Each session is three weeks long, and each day is made up of six periods with three minors and three majors all an hour long. The majors are meant to be a progressive thing, so they're chosen at the start of each session and the kids are supposed to show some sort of improvement. Majors are when the kids will rehearse for one of the 50+ shows they put on each summer, if they choose to be in them. The minors they choose every day at breakfast from a huge list of activities: they could learn to play an instrument, train as a lifeguard, ride a horse, play the guitar, join the circus, sing, do all sorts of dancing, play tennis... Wish I could have come here when I was a kid, it's incredible!

12:45pm Every day we have to:

1. Get the kids up, check they shower and get them to breakfast.
2. Make sure they eat and choose their minors for the day from the printed sheet that comes round.
3. Go back to the bunk with them and check they have everything they need for the day.
4. Make sure they get to their lessons, as well as being at the lessons we're due to teach on time.
5. Teach three lessons in the morning with five-minute breaks in between each one.
6. Get back to our bunk and make sure we have all our bunk campers there.
7. When they're all there, go up to the dining hall for lunch.
8. Make sure they eat enough/not too much.
9. Go back to the bunk and make sure the kids leave with everything they need for the afternoon.
10. Be at our next lesson on time.
11. Teach another three lessons.
12. Go back to the bunk and wait for all the kids.
13. Go up to the dining hall for dinner.
14. Make sure they eat enough/not too much.
15. Go back to the bunk for rest hour – during this time you need to know where your kids are at all times and you should be there for them if they want to talk or need you for any other reason.
16. Get all your bunk kids to the evening activity – make sure they're dressed appropriately for the weather.
17. Go to canteen where the kids dance, chat and eat. One counselor from each bunk has to be in the bunk throughout the evening so the kids always know where they can find someone.
18. If you're on duty you have to stay in the bunk all night now and make sure the kids are in bed by lights out, which is a different time depending on your campers' age.

19. If you're not on duty, then from 9:30pm you have the evening to yourself to do what you like, as long as you're back for 7am to get the kids up for breakfast.

Sounds pretty intense!

1:17pm Just worked out why they waited so long to show me the 'DJ and radio booth'. It's not full of cool decks, flashy lights and mixing gear at all. It's basically a shed structure made from tin sheets, which has enough space to fit five people – at a push. You go through the red door and inside there are two chairs and a desk with a 30cmx30cm mixing deck on and two sets of headphones, and that's it! I've lugged about 200 CDs over to America for this. It actually makes me laugh when I think about how shit it is – I can't show off to my friends back home about this! So glad Bud's going to find me something else to do now.

3pm Eugh, the showers and toilets in the bunk are gross. I thought the shared toilets in my university halls were bad, these are fucking disgusting. We have to clean them thoroughly on our hands and knees today. The toilets are normal toilets, but without a seat and none of the doors actually fit properly. If you're walking through the bathroom you can see into the cubicles through the crack in the door. There's one bathroom between the two adjoining bunks – which is four toilets and six showers between 32 girls. The showers just have a manky old shower curtain across – some not even that – so there's *no* privacy either. There are six sinks; three on each side with a big mirror behind and each bunk has a rack where the girls can put their shampoo and conditioner. We have a little window at each end but no curtains; they both just have netted fly protector. Wow, not looking forward to showering with a load of girls in here, what if they see my bits? Eugh, worse, what if I see theirs?

At breakfast I sat with Emily, Danielle and the other English girls I met on the plane. At the moment everyone seems to be sticking with their nationality, probably because they met on the way over here. In a weird environment like this I guess everyone craves familiarity.

The dining halls are huge and divided into two, one for the younger campers (five to 11) and one for the older ones (12-18). Both are filled with benches and tables set out in rows, just like you see in the high schools on American films. The walls are covered in murals and plaques from years before, and then there's a big run of windows along one side so you can see outside to the tennis courts. At the front of the hall they have big servers and the kitchen staff, who all seem to be Polish, stand behind and plop out the food onto your plate. You can see them rushing around like mad dogs in the kitchen behind. It must be carnage to work in there feeding 300 children and 200ish staff every day for twelve weeks.

6:47pm The camp director Bud has decided I'll work up at visual arts and cover radio for one lesson a day so the other guy can have a break. Now that I've seen the radio/DJ booth, that suits me fine. He took me up to visual arts, which is about a ten-minute walk from my bunk, along the main path, past all the boys bunks and the front office, to meet the boss lady. She seemed really nice and said she was happy to have me on board. Everyone is so welcoming and kind here, I love it.

I sat next to the 'Love Me' trackie bottoms girl from the bus at the visual arts induction, she's actually pretty funny. She was all worked up about how much we're expected to do here, with the bunk duties and all the lessons we have to teach at visual arts.
Her: "Listen to em bangin on, what da fuck? Der gonna work us like dogs and pay us in scraps."

All she wants to do is play on the crazy golf course next to the visual arts building. She came here to be a lifeguard, but has ended up in visual arts and she is *not* happy.

I stayed up at visual arts for the afternoon – the amount of stuff the kids can do is incredible. Painting, drawing, cartooning, sculpture, calligraphy, photography, ceramics, jewellery, silk-screening, weaving, macramé, needlecraft, batik, tie-dye, stained glass, woodwork, video and leather craft, wow. And they expect *me* to teach it. Oh dear, need to brush up on my blagging skills, but I'm definitely excited to get to play with it all.

Visual arts is set out like a sweatshop. It's in an L-shaped shed with just a few exterior walls and pillars holding it up so the fresh air can breeze through. There are one or two long tables in each department with pew-style benches either side, and a cupboard with supplies. It goes from leather at one end, through to woodwork at the other. There's another visual arts shed down a steep hill where they have silk-screening, photography and video.

We wanted to refresh the décor for this year, so we decided

to paint colourful silhouettes – like the iPod adverts – on the walls. I did a handstand against one of them and the trackie bottoms girl, Cara, drew around me. I spent the afternoon painting it in and they actually look pretty good.

9:17pm Had some blue cake at dinner, very weird. It actually turned my mouth blue with all the food colouring. Hope that's not what the kids eat when they arrive.

Had another staff meeting in the Kennedy Theatre near our bunk after lunch. Earl said another load of counselors would arrive in three weeks, as there are more kids in second and third sessions, and apparently this will be a relatively quiet one. Some kids stay on for two, three or even four sessions, while others just come for one.

Bud explained the head counselors to us. There are six on camp covering different ages. They're not that much older than me, but I think they've all been coming to camp for a while. Bud said if anything gets complicated in any way, or we're having any problems, we're to go to them. They're trained to deal with the kids and the parents and they'll know if the kids have any special requirements and pass on what we need to know. We're there to be mothers, sisters, friends, counselors and teachers, but if things get tricky, ask them.

Bud: "You're in for a great summer. You'll work harder than you ever have, but you'll look back when it's over and wish you could do it all over again."

Everything sounds brilliant – ahhh, I'm so excited! Oh, they also told us that if any of the kids are feeling homesick they have a camp mum here who's literally just hired to give the campers love and hugs. How odd. He also said we need to take the beds by the doors and sleep with one eye open to make sure the campers don't go out at night. I'll make sure they don't try anything on my watch.

11:33pm I've been a bit confused about this whole 'shop' business. At first I thought people were talking about actual shops, but I realised that's what they call the departments, like rock shop, costume shop and magic shop. I'm glad I managed to work that one out without asking anyone, could've been embarrassing.

I'm going to try and get to sleep again in this cold and desolate bunk now. Not really made friends with my bunk buddies yet, I haven't seen them around in the day and so now it's just awkward in the evening. They don't seem too keen on me, I'm trying to tell myself not to be paranoid, but I am. Why don't they speak to me? I thought we'd all be best friends by now, working together towards this 'best summer of our lives' we're supposed to be having.

Wednesday 8th June

11:12am Nope, didn't sleep again last night, but got some *very* good news this morning: I'm in the wrong bunk, wooo! I was out of there like a shot when the head counselor told me. I did not like the atmosphere in there at all; I knew it wasn't right for me. I should've been next door in B, and I'd gone into A, silly me. Here I found my real bunk buddies: Jude from New Zealand and Rebecca from the Channel Islands. I liked them straight away. I'm so grateful I'm not stuck with those girls next door for the entire summer; I honestly don't know how I would've coped.

Rebecca's been to Rockbear before; she's been telling Jude and me stories all morning about last year. Most interestingly, she told us about all the famous people's kids that go here. Apparently you can get tipped up to $1000 per session, well happy with that! Rebecca: "Be careful though. They'll sack you instantly if they don't like you, so make sure you suck up to all the bosses."

That scared me a bit; imagine going home after getting fired from camp. It would be so embarrassingly awful to have to go back early.

Rebecca teaches up in visual arts like me. She looks cool with all her jewellery and boho style. I've asked her so many questions about camp I hope I'm not getting on her nerves. She took me around with her while she went to see who'd come back to camp from last year. There are loads of returnees actually – that must be a good sign – and she's friends with them all. I liked hanging out with her, it made it so much easier to meet and chat to people. She's really pretty, not like a pop star or anything, but in a more unique and interesting way. She's got a speech impediment that makes her say 'Webecca', which made me laugh – she finds it funny too though, so that's ok.

Jude is running the fencing department – she's some sort of champion of it in New Zealand and a qualified schoolteacher at home by day. She wanted a year's break to travel and thought this would be the perfect way to put her skills to use. She's really friendly and interested in what I've got to say, which is always nice.

4:16pm 'Love Me' trackies girl, Cara, is *so* funny. It's her Irish accent; it makes anything she says ten times funnier. I asked her about being a lifeguard – seeing as that's what she came here to do – apparently they didn't tell her she needed a qualification and didn't check. Then when she got here they asked for her certificate, which she obviously didn't have, so they stuck her up at visual arts. Every time I see her she's got a sweeping brush in her hand – think that's her non-committal contribution to the setting up process in the hope they'll let her at the water.

7:12pm It's so surreal to actually be here. I remember wanting to do it after I finished school, but I didn't want to come by myself and my best friend wasn't 18 until July. Then last year I just worked in an office all summer and blitzed the cash on driving lessons and a mad week in Ibiza at the end of it. When I turned 20 in October I was determined to do something more fun with this summer. I've never been anywhere by myself before, and not really even been abroad that much. I went to France with my family once, Ibiza, and then to Kavos on a girlie holiday two years ago, but that's it for my jet setting. It's weird to be in America on my own, quite impressed with myself though.

I'm scared about the kids arriving in a few days. I'm not one of those people who grew up with kids everywhere and I've never really even hung out with seven to 17-year-olds, apart from when I was one. I've just got one older brother. I guess there are my cousins, but that's different and I only see them twice a year, if that. This summer is definitely going to be a challenge, but I'm excited!

Thursday 9th June

12:17pm I've only been at camp for four days and I can already say my big plan for a three-month detox isn't going to work out. Last night there was a party for all the counselors up at the Golf Club – the GC for short. The place probably serves no more than 10 people a night for the rest of the year, but every summer they let all the counselors from Rockbear go up. They must make an *absolute* mint out of us. It's about a ten-minute walk away from the camp car park, up a very steep hill. From the outside it looks like some sort of ranch nestled in a golf course. Climb up the wooden steps and you're in the main room, which is decked out like a log cabin about 10 metres squared with chairs, tables and bar stools dotted around. The walls are covered in golfing pictures and there's a stag's head stuck above the bar – pretty sure it's real. A balcony runs all the way around the main room, big enough for chairs and tables to admire the course from, and round the back the terrace is even bigger. It's perfect for chilling out under the stars with a beverage or four.

Everyone was drinking pitchers of beer – that's the only way they serve it – shots, or jugs of cocktails. I had so much fun just listening to music and chatting to everyone. Some people seemed really awkward there, but I was in my element trying to sniff out all the other boozehounds. Danielle is definitely one of them, we were chatting for ages. I love her soft Brummy accent – reminds me of home. She's got her tongue pierced, but Earl will go nuts if he sees it, so she has to talk with tight lips when she's around him. I also got chatting to this guy Jamie who works in video. He's from New York and works as a news journalist for a local TV station there. How cool is that? Tried to get him to find me some work experience, but I think he thought I was joking; I'll work on him.

Pete who works up at the stables with the horses is pretty cool too; he's gorgeous, tall and from Formby near Liverpool so he has a beautiful accent too. Shame he's gay. He's really funny and I got on with him straight away. It's so cool there are horses on camp; I hope counselors are allowed to take them for a ride.

I've met some really inspirational people here so far. I actually feel quite embarrassed about how little I've travelled when I talk to everyone. I've just grown up in the same small village all my life. I went to infants, juniors and high school there and spent every weekend in the local town, sporadically going to the nearest city when I felt like an adventure. Then I went to the bright lights of Sheffield for university and that's it. Some people here have been coming since they were 18 and do it every summer while fitting in cool stuff – like ski seasons and language camp – the rest of the year. I wish I'd had the balls to come by myself as soon as I was old enough. Better make the most of it now I guess!

6:16pm I'm slightly horrified at how shabby the camp is. I've been going around pulling nails out from the wood and fitting the windowpanes back in properly. I guess it's just from the close up over winter, but it's a bit worrying that the kids will be here in just two days. I've swept and scrubbed the bunk so hard – it's as clean as it'll ever be.

We got our camp-issue t-shirts today – I love them! They gave us a brown polo neck and a fitted purple cotton tee to wear on changeover days when the new kids come. If we ever go on days out with the kids we have to wear them too. Think everyone was a bit over excited though and all the counselors are strutting around with 'Camp Rockbear' written across their chest.

My bunkmate Rebecca introduced me to her best mate from last year Jo; she'll be working up at visual arts with us too and runs the jewellery department. Both of them have come to Rockbear for the past four years – which means they've now spent a whole year of their lives at camp, wow. The Australian school year runs January to December, so Jo has pretty much fucked up her schooling especially so she can come here.

Jo: "Where else do you have your best friends on your doorstep, do you get to behave like a kid all day, have everything paid for and work out in the fresh air all day long?"

Good point well-made Jo. I like her.

8pm Cara's managed to charm some 'Camp Rockbear'-emblazoned tartan pyjama bottoms from the front office to replace her 'Love Me' trackies, thank god. She's well proud of herself. I'm sure the guy at reception is into her, and the lucky gap between her teeth did its work. There's loads of Camp Rockbear branded stuff up there for sale – bags, swimsuits, hoodies, trousers. I guess they're cool while you're here, but I couldn't imagine wearing them out and about at home. Maybe back home the kids are really proud of the camp they go to; it's probably some sort of status symbol.

Friday 10th June

7:31am Every morning the sound of bells over the loudspeaker wakes us up at 7:30am, and then this...

Loudspeaker: "Eeeeeeeeeeeevvverybody up, up, up! It's time to riiiise and shiiine... It's a beautiful day on the Rockbear campus..."

Bud doesn't seem to care what it's actually like outside when he says this – he'll never make it as a weatherman.

8pm Went to Kingfisher Falls today with all the other counselors for a day off before all the kids arrive tomorrow. It's a big shallow lake with a waterfall and natural rock pools about 40 minutes' drive from camp. We took a load of food and drink and a stereo, and just hung out there all day to chill. I started to feel a bit homesick. I think it's just because I was tired – the past five days of camp have been pretty intense with all the cleaning, new people and meeting after meeting.

I felt a bit left out too. Everyone seems to be friends already and I didn't know what to do to get involved. I sat around with a few other outcasts – Emily and Cara and a few others – while everyone else was in this big rock pool drinking beers and having a laugh. I think they all came last year so know each other already, but I still felt like a loser perched on the edge. Me, Cara, Emily and a few of the other girls I met on the plane went for a walk in the forest, and it actually ended up being a good laugh getting to know them better. I guess I need to remember it just takes time to make friends.

Last night I went back to one of the guys from tennis' bunk. I didn't think he was that fit at the time, he was coming on to me and I fended him off, but I'm regretting it a bit now. Everyone was all over him at Kingfisher Falls and the girls keep saying how fit he is. There's nothing like a bit of jealousy to make you like someone.

Anyway, enough of that. When we got back I went up to visual arts and our schedules were ready. This is going to be my day in session one...

- 7:30am wake up
- 8:00am breakfast
- 9:30am free
- 10:30am break
- 10:45am stained glass minor
- 11:45am break
- 12noon radio minor
- 1:00pm meet the girls at the bunk
- 1:15pm lunch
- 2:15pm ceramics major
- 3:15pm break
- 3:30pm crafts minor
- 4:30pm break

- 4:45pm creative writing major
- 5:45pm break
- 6:00pm dinner
- 7:00pm rest hour
- 8:00pm evening activity
- 9:30pm either on duty or free for the night.

We get two days off per three-week session. Obviously all the staff can't be off on the same day so three quarters of the staff have the day off together – known as 'normal day off' or 'lazy day' to the kids. The other quarter of staff – the alternate day staff – stay on camp with the kids and play, or take them to the cinema, or whatever Earl and Bud have decided we're doing that day. There are no lessons or majors or minors. It's a chance for the kids to relax or learn their lines for their productions.

Alternate day staff – which is me – then get another day off that week to do what they want. This basically means that alternate day staff have four days off per session and the normal day staff have two. We get to hang out with the kids when they go to the cinema on lazy day *and* get a day off with the other alternate day counselors too. Sounds good to me!

We can do whatever we want on our free lessons. Bud said to make the most of being on camp and to try everything, so I will. During the week all the counselors have to share duties. This session I have to stay in the bunk on Friday and Sunday nights and then on a Wednesday go and DJ up at canteen. The other four nights I'm free to do what I like. GC here I come!

I'm well excited to be teaching so many random things. I need to do some planning for my creative writing major tomorrow. I have to show how I think the kids will progress through the three-week course.

I still don't feel like I've really slept since I left home, probably too excited. We've got electricity now, but the beds are so uncomfortable and it's still absolutely freezing at night. There's never going to be any heating; I guess it'll be better when we have more people in the bunk though. In the middle of the night I went over to the cubby where I keep all my clothes and put absolutely everything I owned on. I was still cold though. At least I learnt from my last bunk not to choose a bed near the bathroom, Rebecca must be freezing over there.

I really hope I'm in for a good summer. There's been such a big run up and drum roll to tomorrow. I've spent the last six months being excited for it and the last week preparing. The camp's looking pretty good now, the nails have been pulled out, the bunks are sparkling clean, there's a fresh lick of paint here and there and I think, we're ready. One more sleep until the kids arrive!

Saturday 11th June

10am Ahh, I'm SUPER nervous. Me, Jude and Rebecca are waiting in the bunk together ready to welcome the kids. We've put signs up saying 'Welcome to F13B' and made glittery paper nametags for our beds too. What do you say to 13-year-old girls? I'm trying to remember what I was into at that age. It's school year nine in England: I was pretty naughty. I remember in year nine getting my friends' older sister to buy us some hooch for another friends' sleepover. That was a fun night. I was on the verge of going to under-18 discos, drinking mixes from my parents' alcohol cupboard in the queue and snogging all the boys, but I think that was more likely year 10. Oh god, I hope they're not like that. This could be karma coming back round to bite me, and it will definitely hurt. Right, better look lively; they could walk in any second.

Sunday 12th June

9:45am Crazy yet cringey is how I'd describe yesterday. The girls seem so young, not like I remember myself at 13. I showed them where to put their stuff and let them choose a bed. We'd already been told that if they wanted the beds we'd chosen we'd have to move. I'm glad they didn't turf me out, that would not have been good for trying to show them who's boss. They all seem quite shy. It might be because their parents were there and being really embarrassing though – one parent told me to make sure I kiss her little one goodnight and another was describing the best bedtime routine to get them to sleep. Jeez, I hope they're good fun so I can rip them for that later.

The parents scared me more than the kids – I knew they were sizing me up to check I was suitable to look after their precious little ones for the next three weeks. It must be worrying for them though; they don't know anything about me. I was a bit of a pathetic mute, I couldn't think of anything to say to them. I just kept nodding and smiling, like an idiot.

Me, Jude and Rebecca went up to lunch in shifts. Some of the counselors sat with the parents in the dining hall, but I found Danielle instead and we both sat there overwhelmed and shell-shocked. We barely said a word to each other, definitely not normal for us. My campers all look the same – tiny little things with long big dark hair and deep-set eyes – how am I ever going to learn their names? I'll start with the non-Jewish looking ones first: blonde Joey and chubby Keakuki.

Most of the girls have put up a few family photographs around their beds. I tried to make friends with them by asking who was who on the pictures.

Camper: "Mum, dad, my brother."

Hmmm, don't think that's going to work for a lengthy getting-to-know-you conversation; maybe they can sense my fear.

I've already noticed how prepared and regimented my bunkmate Jude is in everything she does. Trust her to follow the CCUSA guidelines to bring a few photos to show what life is like in your own country. I don't think the kids were too interested though. Jude's actually really starting to grate on me; everything has to be just so and she bosses me around all the time. I know she's a schoolteacher at home so obviously knows more about looking after kids than I do, but her 'helpful' comments are just annoying. If she patronises me in front of the kids I'll be raging. Everything you've done, she's always done something better. Her voice is irritating too; she shrieks and squeals every time she opens her mouth. Still another three months of camp to go though, I need to calm down, shut up and deal with it.

Jude and Rebecca had to leave the bunk to go and help in their departments, so I was left with the kids. I really didn't know what to say. We were all sat on our bunks and just looking at each other.

Me (super enthusiastically): "So, which shows are you going to audition for?"

Camper: "Dunno."

Other camper: "I'm not really into acting."

They're a tough crowd, but they seem nice enough. I know it will be better with time, but I just want us all to have fun together. I chatted awkwardly to whoever was in the bunk while the others went to auditions and tryouts. My approach basically consisted of phony compliments about their possessions and asking whether they'd been to camp before. I actually bored myself.

There were just six minors yesterday, no majors, so the kids could use the minors to audition for the shows, get assessed for swimming and settle in to camp life. I've seen other kids around camp nervously walking around reciting their audition pieces and warbling to warm up their voices. I'm in the set of *Fame*.

7:49pm Had to teach my first lesson today – stained glass with Cara. I do not know a *thing* about stained glass, only that it looks pretty in churches, and neither does Cara. Instead we sat around playing getting-to-know-you games. Whoever was holding the Stanley knife had to say their name and give an interesting fact about themselves. It generally ended up being where they were from or what school they went to – I was hoping it would be a way for me to find out which kids had the famous parents. Some of the kids seem so lifeless and droopy with no spark in their eyes, while others are up and excited about anything you say. We definitely need to get the glass and wood ready for them next time; I think they enjoyed it though. I was pretty nervous –
I was glad Cara was there to lighten the mood.

Next I had to teach radio. I felt pretty stupid as it took me about five minutes to explain what to do – and the kids knew anyway – and then I just had to sit there. I found it hard to make conversation with the three boys, they weren't interested in me, all they wanted to do was to see how loud the speakers would go.

The rest of the day went alright – no one came to creative writing so I just sat there playing music. I wanted to go back to the bunk, but I was too scared in case I got told off for skiving. In ceramics I just had to sit there with the naughty kids while this other woman taught the rest of them. Then I had crafts with Cara – we just gave the kids some glitter, card and pens and told them to make signs for their beds in their bunks. Not sure why the visual arts boss has put Cara and me together to teach – think it's pretty obvious we don't know anything.

Monday 13th June

9:47am Wow, the queue at meal times for the nurse is snaked! She sits at the front of the dining hall with a massive stack of drugs doling them out. So many kids are on Ritalin or anti-depressants or some other mood-enhancer or downer drug, it's incredible. I really think the parents should take a look at the breakfast their kids are eating first, before pumping them full of medication. There's this fluorescent cereal called Fruit Loops, which must have every food colouring going in it. No wonder the kids are bouncing off the walls and crashing back down. Cara's in a bunk with the seven to eight-year-olds and she's got this girl who eats them colour by colour super-fast, completely focused with her head down to the bowl. She doesn't even come up for air – it's amazing to watch.

It's going well with my girls. I'm still a bit unsure of what to say to them, but we bonded this morning over cleaning the bunk. Once breakfast is done we go back to the bunk and after a mad rush for the showers, we have a cleaning rota to follow every day. The toilets and showers need to be cleaned, all the floors need to be swept and mopped, and the cubbies where they keep their clothes have to be neat and tidy. I demonstrated each station by messing around and doing a little dance with the sweeping brush, basically just being a bit of an idiot, but it made them laugh. The girls are all so sweet and lovely they actually seemed excited to do it. The head counselor told us we were the tidiest bunk today on her daily inspection – I'm going to find it difficult to keep up with them.

Five of the girls are friends from home, but they're really open and welcoming to the other girls who aren't. They're so different from anyone I knew at 13. It was all about cliques, superficial friendships and bitching at my school, I can't imagine these lovely girls there.

I'm on my free lesson now. It feels weird to be in the bunk with no one else here. Our bunk is near the canteen and dining hall, but away from all the shops so it's really quiet in the day. I've just had a shower. I'm getting used to the grim cubicles now, although I'm going to stick with showering in my free for now, rather than when all the kids are about. I'm sure in a few days I won't even notice the grime and the fact everyone can see you, but I'm still feeling a bit uncomfortable now. I'm going to check the girls' photos to see if I can find something else to talk to them about when they get back. Sneaky me.

2pm I love taking the register at the start of the lesson, it was always my favourite part of playing teachers as a kid. I'm such a geek. Cara and me were more prepared for stained glass today, we got some squares of wood, a few sheets of glass, grout and some Stanley knives and we attempted to make a lesson out of it. We smashed the glass up for the kids with a little hammer and they fitted it all together again and stuck it to the wood. Then they smooth the grout over to fill in the gaps with their fingertips. I cannot believe Earl and Bud actually let this happen. I'm sure when their rich, American, lawsuit-loving parents see nothing but broken glass glued onto wood they'll be onto their lawyers. I keep slicing my fingertips myself. Hmmm, actually, I wonder if I could sue? I need to find out if any of my kids have lawyers for parents, they can be my favourites.

7:11pm I'm still feeling a bit shy around some of the counselors. I feel like I've kind of missed my window to talk to them and it's a bit awkward. I don't know why: it's stupid and I can't spend the rest of camp avoiding them, but I just feel silly and shy that they won't want to talk to me if I do start up a conversation. Wish I was more confident like the kids; they're all best friends already.

12:56am Once a week at midnight we have a weekly staff meeting. I was excited about it before and thought it sounded cool, but I've just been to one and it was horrible. We put the kids to bed early and the head counselors patrol the bunks while we venture down to the Regal Theatre, which is right over the other side of camp behind visual arts and by the swimming pool. It's a long walk and the clear mountain air means it's freezing. Everyone is so tired and the last thing you want is to sit on a pew listening to Earl bang on for an hour. He said how well camp was going and to be prepared for the new counselors coming in a few days, because camp will be a lot busier. He said he's already caught a few girls going awol at night so we need to keep an eye out. I'm sure my girls would never do that – they're all snuggly asleep by 11pm.

Apparently last night two of the waterfront staff got caught shagging in the lifeboat shack by their boss, haha, gutted. From all the rumours and what I've seen with my own eyes this camp is absolute filth for both counselors and campers. It's like some free loving cult up in the New York mountains.

Tuesday 14th June

11pm All us alternate dayers went shopping to the local city, Truhampton, while the normal-day staff stayed on camp to carry on with the day as usual. It was weird – I kind of didn't want to go. It feels like I'm missing out on bonding time with the girls – like when you have a new baby and you have to be around for the early days, otherwise you inflict irreparable damage on your lifelong relationship with them – or something like that.

I had fun shopping though. The camp driver, John, dropped us off and we just hung out in the mall all day. They've got some really cool surf and skate type shops here, there's one called Hot Topic that sells the coolest t-shirts and random crap. I need to stay away or I'll be spending all my non-existent money in there.

When I got back Rebecca, Jude and the girls were all in the bunk laughing and chatting – I was gutted. It felt like a punch to the heart. I wanted to be the one that got on with them the best and I really didn't want to miss out on anything. Oh well, I'll just have to try harder tomorrow I guess.

Wednesday 15th June

5:16pm No one's turned up to my creative writing lesson again – very sad. No one cares. At least it means another free for me though, woo!

Cara and me have quickly become really good friends. As well as stained glass we also have to teach craft together and neither of us has a clue. A bunch of seven year olds want to learn craft from us two – a wannabe lifeguard and DJ? Haha, unlucky. I had a brainwave today though – we had some sponge heads for the mops so we chopped them up for the kids and gave them some eyes, pipe cleaners, pens, glue and felt, and showed them how to make a SpongeBob Squarepants. The kids *absolutely* loved it. I don't think the visual arts boss was too impressed though. God, she's a weird one.

There's this camper from Hawaii in my bunk, Keakuki. I'm so fascinated by the fact she's from Hawaii – I just thought it was where rich people went on holiday. She's very sweet, sometimes. At other times she's totally nuts and just goes crazy at us, screaming and screeching about where her top is, or what some other kid has said to her. I'd say she feels like the odd one out with all these skinny little Jewish girls though, she's probably twice the size of them and twice as ugly. She's so loud as well. She seems to have taken a liking to me, whenever she sees me around camp she just screeches, "Luuccccyyyy!" and runs over to me for a hug nearly bowling me over. I guess I should be grateful; she's horrible to Jude.

9:16pm Food here is *weird*: deep-fried cauliflower, toxic-coloured cereal, minging squeezy cheese, disgusting sugary bread, but oooo homemade cookies with chocolate chips today. Loved them. There are soda dispensers up there with unlimited refills, so as well as the sugar and e number-filled food the kids get high on coke too.

Evening activity tonight was a song recital. Some of these kids make me cringe they're such nerds. Anyone who was in the recital has been walking around camp today with a sign round their necks saying 'vocal rest' and not speaking. When they do sing it's operatic and they flutter their eyelids like they're having a bit of a seizure when they hit the high notes. Didn't like it.

2isham Went up to the GC tonight. Cara turned up in her pyjamas, again. What a hero. I snogged Tim from rock shop – he's a right fitty and he's well into little old me, woohoo! He's got cool shaggy hair, a buff bod and such a cute smile. My bunkmate Rebecca got with his ugly mate and Danielle was getting it on with her climbing wall boss. I'm sure that will be fun for her in the morning.

In the evenings the dining hall is open until about 2am for the counselors in case we're hungry. There are loads of cereals and breads out for us, which is great if you can't be arsed to walk up the big hill to the GC, but want to hang out away from the kids. When we got back from the GC tonight me and Cara went to see if anyone was in there. There were about 15 counselors all having a cereal fight; obviously we got stuck right in there. I stood on one of the tables and spun round sprinkling coco pops everywhere, then Cara copied me and we ended up just chucking the little variety pack boxes at each other, using people for shields. We're going to get our arses whipped tomorrow, but it was so much fun trashing the place.

I love everyone here so much. Not just because I've had a drink, but because I genuinely feel like I've met my soul mates. We have such a laugh – Cara and me, gay horsey Pete and me, everyone and me... – no one could ever understand this experience unless they actually have it I don't know how I'll even begin to explain it all to my friends at home. We're a team here, we support each other and we know exactly what each other is going through so we can sympathise with each other's camp troubles. I like it when we get together and discuss tactics for keeping the kids in line, and I like it even better when we come together and DRINK.

Thursday 16th June

8:02am Eugh, waking up at the crack of dawn with a hangover is definitely not fun when you have to get the kids up too, especially when it hits you that you have to teach for the next eight hours. That fucking loudspeaker is making my ears bleed. I need to stop getting so pissed at the GC. I can't deal with the kids in my lessons when I'm like this. All of a sudden they're five times more annoying.

9:15am My bunk's bench is quite far back in the dining hall, so every morning I have to walk past all the other bunks' tables to get to the food. Danielle's bunk sits at the front and every morning she trills, 'You alriiight' at me in her Brummy tones as I go past. Pretty funny, although she didn't say it with her usual enthusiasm today and she looks rough as. Maybe she should give up those late night shots too.

Jude is so annoyingly proactive; I knew she would be as soon as I saw her. She's one of those perky people – always wearing a North Face jacket or body warmer – and ready for action at a second's notice. She likes order and she doesn't drink. You wouldn't catch her crawling up the steps to the bunk at three in the morning. We're two very different people, and she needs to chill out if we're going to make it through the summer.

6:42pm The woman who leads ceramics next door to us in stained glass must've been bought in especially for her 'skills', it's definitely not for her award-winning personality. She's so strict, yet really dithery at the same time. As soon as she has a naughty kid they run rings round her and she doesn't know what to do. I have to teach ceramics with her every day and in the lessons I've had with her so far, she's just made me sit at a table with the naughty kids expecting me to sort them out while she works with all the nice ones. I'd never used clay in my life before I came here, so I guess it's for the best, in a way. She spends her time firing up the kiln – she's always going on about that fucking kiln – and getting the clay ready for the kids. She's another one who doesn't appreciate mine and Cara's sense of humour and play – 'fuckin dry shite', are the three most obvious words to describe her.

7:17pm Before I came to camp I was worried about not being liked by the kids, but now one of my campers absolutely worships me and it's really getting on my nerves. She tracks me down around camp and wants to hug and touch me all the time. I do feel sorry for her, she told me she's the most unpopular kid at school and I'm pretty sure she's not exaggerating. She's so gangly and doofus-like. She's also one of those sickly children with a permanent cold. She starts every sentence with an emphatic 'so' – which really gets on my nerves too. When she wants to ask me something it's, "Lucy, can I ask a question?" Argh, why can't she just ask me the question first time round?

There are definitely some *very* odd children here. One of Cara's campers has become obsessed with her too; she comes up to visual arts and makes all this crap to give her. She makes hearts with her name in and leaves them on Cara's pillow. Cara is not impressed. She's not warm in the huggy, lovey dovey way – like she wouldn't give a child a big hug or be tender with them if they were sick or anything – her way of being warm is more in the fact that she's fun and makes the kids laugh and feel at ease. She doesn't like the weird kids, or the ugly ones, or the fat kids either. She told me if she had an ugly, fat kid she'd give it up for adoption. A few things I've learned about Cara so far include:

- Her 30-second mood swings – occasionally she'll stomp around ranting about the 'fuckin dry shites'. Then the next minute, she'll be laughing – throwing her head back and cracking up.
- When she laughs she does it heartily, slapping her hands on her knees and bending over double with her mouth wide open. Her whole body jolts.
- Actually that's another thing – she's extreme. She'll either love something, "dat's da fuckin' bollocks", or hate it "dat's fuckin' shite", and the same goes for people.

- She has this odd habit of always pulling at her nose – like she's wiping imaginary bogies, or she's just snorted some drugs. Pretty sure she hasn't, although she is *very* perky.
- She's fucking funny.

7:34pm Earlier today in ceramics I was put in charge of this seven-year-old whose parents died in 9/11, four years ago now. Obviously I felt really sorry for him, and he's the cutest kid in the world too with big brown eyes and a perfect little smile complete with dimples. We were just mucking about, but I got him all hyped up and excited by being silly and making faces with the clay – he got giddy and ran off. He was legging it around the miniature golf course, and of course I couldn't keep up, which he found hilarious. Twenty minutes later I managed to catch up with him/he got bored and he decided he wanted to play with water. It's been a cold day, but obviously, cute kid, parents dead, what can you say? So we did. At the end of the lesson I went to clear his stuff away and as I'm bending over he comes and wrings out a *freezing* cold sponge over my head. Then he proudly does it to himself, and just ends up in fits of giggles rolling around on the floor. He was laughing so much he got the hiccups. He is *so* cute; love him. There are some adorable kids here, but plenty of little shits too.

11:49pm In the evenings they have 'canteen', which is where I DJ. It's just a big shed at the top of camp past the tennis courts and near the dining hall. There's endless ice cream and pizza to fatten the kids up before sleep, it's unbelievable. The queue snakes around and the kids stand in line waiting for ice cream while shoving pizza in their mouths. The counselors making it in the kitchen can't work fast enough. This goes on for about an hour and a half depending on the age of your kids. Thirty minutes after going up there Cara has to round up her little ones and get them back to bed, but they're all super high on sugar, cheese and party music – nightmare. Some of them just aren't satisfied with all the pizza and sugar and so hit up the vending machines on the way out too.

Friday 17th June

7:16pm First lazy day today! Normally there will be two lazy days per session, but because this is a shorter session we've only got one. All of us alternate-day staff wore our Camp Rockbear t-shirts for their first outing and took the kids to see *Star Wars II: The Phantom Menace.* It felt a bit wrong on such a sunny day but hey ho, we're always outside anyway. The rest of the counselors with normal-day off went to NYC for the day.

We got on the big yellow school bus and headed off to the nearest cinema in the local town Winkworth 20 minutes away, singing all the way. The cinema is really old-school – more like a regal theatre with an ornate ceiling, luxurious red seating and opulent curtains over the screen that dramatically opened when the film started. In the foyer they had popcorn made in a carnival popcorn-maker and saltwater taffy, which I found out is absolutely disgusting. The kids were going crazy for it though. It's such a nightmare/laugh to get 300 campers into the screen with the snacks they want, most of them had eaten the candy by the time the film started and wanted more. The counselors had to budge the kids up to sit sporadically among them to stop any sexiness or naughtiness. I've never seen a *Star Wars* film before and probably won't ever again – it was boring, but I did miss the hour in the middle when I was asleep. When I woke up all the kids around me were laughing and I was covered in popcorn. Pretty sure I'd been snoring and dribbling.

10:16pm I hung out in the bunk with the girls when we got back and chatted about school and what they wanted to do when they graduated. They have to go to university for so many years here, it's crazy. And it's *so* expensive – tens of thousands of dollars. That's why parents start saving as soon as they're born and why getting scholarships, like you see in the movies, is so important. These girls are amazing; I bet they'll do well in whatever they decide to do.

I'm managing to cope with the shower situation. The girls don't seem bothered about privacy, so I guess I shouldn't feel weird about it either. It is a bit odd when I'm showering and they're all around getting ready and brushing their teeth. You can't help but see people in the shower when you walk in the bathroom because of the shit curtains and mirror positioning.

I'm amazed at how well I'm getting on with the kids. I've worked out that in lessons all you have to do is talk to them and be jolly and they're your friend. Well, the younger ones anyway. Some of the older ones are a bit harder to crack, but you just have to keep talking to them and show that you're fun. I'm really happy with my relationship with the girls in my bunk. I came in earlier from being at the bunk next door and two of them got up and started hugging me asking where I'd been and saying how much they missed me. I know they were joking, but it was nice. I never thought I'd get on with them this well.

It seems a bit harsh that they don't let the kids phone home for the first week of camp. I can see why they do it – they're more likely to be homesick if they speak to their parents – but it seems a bit mean. Today was the first day they were allowed to do it and when we got back from the cinema the kids were fighting each other to get to the front of the queue up at the front office.

Had to listen to the string orchestra earlier for evening activity. If there's a musical instrument I hate, it's got to be a violin. Bloody racket.

Saturday 18th June

1:57pm The girl from Brisbane I met on the plane, Emily, and me have become really good friends. Her and Cara are in a bunk together. It's just on the other side of the dividing hedges to mine, in the mixed section near the volleyball court.

Emily's really easy to talk to, she's got these beautiful big eyes that just make her look constantly happy and excited. Me and her went to check out the circus in our free this morning up behind visual arts. Hmmm, not the most welcoming of staff, they obviously didn't want us there. I had a go on the trapeze anyway; it was amazing swinging through the air. Hoops hang down from the ceiling like on *Gladiators* when they used to have to swing from them and wrestle each other down. There are silks to climb up and loads of trampolines and gymnastic equipment, it's amazing. These kids are so lucky they get to try all this stuff out; most people never get to play on a circus trapeze. It amazes me at breakfast when the kids are choosing minors and they ask if they can just 'stay in the bunk'. I feel like an old woman when I tell them to make the most of this opportunity.

Me: "I didn't have all this when I was younger, you should think yourselves lucky and do everything you can."

Calm down grandma.

5:15pm No one's come to my creative writing class again. Now, shall I tell someone I'm free or just keep quiet and go back to bed? Hmmmm, choices, choices.

I love where my bed is in the bunk. I'm above an empty bed so it's easy to get up and down, and it's next to the door for fresh air and easy access when I'm coming in pissed from the GC. Oh, and it's as far away from the smelly bathroom as you can get. Sharing a room is cool, I like having the campers to talk to. I always wanted a sister when I was growing up, and now it's as if I've got 13, even if Jude is really annoying. I've put loads of photos of my friends up on the wall by my bed and all my cosmetics and knick-knacks are lined up on the shelf above. I've bagged the drawer underneath my bunk beds for my clothes too, so I hope no one decides they want to sleep on the bottom. I love how it's my own private area up top, when you're on a bottom bunk people can always see you and they sit on your bed. Not up here though.

I'm getting on really well with Rebecca too. We can just sit and chill and chat, and it feels like I've known her for ages. She's really interesting and clever – she's reading American Studies at King's College London and from all her travelling it just seems like she knows loads about the world. I want to live in London when I finish university, I think. Jude's dull; she's really moany at the kids and just a bit of a drip. Unfortunately, I think she might have missed out on a sense of humour at birth too. I'm having such a good time, I feel like when I get back home I'm going to be just like the girl from the *American Pie* film; "This one time, at band camp..."

The little boy who threw the water on me the other day was chasing me around the visual arts area earlier and play-threatening me with a golf stick. Haven't done so much exercise for ages, it was pretty funny. He was having a great time just giggling and trying to run. I loved seeing him so happy. He must have been through so much with his parents. There are quite a few kids here whose parents died in 9/11 – Earl gets them here on scholarship.

I had a go driving a gator earlier, it's like a golf cart crossed with a little tractor. Bud didn't seem too impressed when I crunched my way down the big hill by visual arts though, especially when the back of it hit the floor and the wheels crunched. Oops, I just trundled off like nothing had happened, la la la.

11.13pm When you're DJing in canteen in the evening, the kids come up to you with pizza and ice cream all over their faces shouting and spitting at you to play their favourite song. It's so gross. They ask me for Happy Birthday shout-outs to their friends too – this is when I know I've made it in life. From the DJ box there's nothing to look at but the kids, so I've made a few notes:

- The super nerds hang out by the vending machines looking uncomfortable. Either they're just there for the sweets, pizza and ice cream, and genuinely don't care about the opposite sex or the music or what they're wearing. Or they just hope that one day they'll turn up to the disco and suddenly fit in.
- All but one or two of the older kids are said 'super nerds'; I guess all the cool ones sacked off summer camp at 16.
- The 'pretty, cool girls' are always late – they've been in their bunks trying on clothes and deciding what to wear. When they do arrive they divide, some just look pretty on the side trying to entice the boys, while others get up and bust out a few 'sexy' moves to the music, usually *Don't Cha* by the Pussycat Dolls. The kids are obsessed with that song. It's a bit weird watching the 12-year-olds thrusting their fannies into each other, I feel scared for my not yet conceived child that this is the world I'll be bringing them into.
- The five to nine-year-old girls try to imitate the older ones, with disturbing results.
- Most of the boys just run around trying to get the attention of the pretty girls. The rest of them are too busy playing airplanes, or wandering around in circles making themselves dizzy and staring at the ceiling.
- The camp is united in their love for the *Cha Cha Slide* song. They squeal with delight when they hear the intro and they know all the moves. I could play that all night and they'd love it. A few of them think they look really good dancing to it – but they don't.

They're basically choosing between music, food and the opposite sex. Give them a few years and they'll learn how to divide their time between them all.

My campers just come up for some pizza, have a giggle together and then go back to the bunk. If I'm in the DJ booth they always drop off some pizza for me, and take a piece back to the bunk for whoever's on duty. Love them.

Sunday 19th June

12:16pm Only one kid has turned up to radio today. He's happy enough working his way through the CDs, I'll leave him to it.

Random passing kids: "SpongeBob Squarepants. SpongeBob Squarepants."

All they want to do when they see Cara and me is to make a SpongeBob Squarepants. They're so cute. The visual arts boss told us we're not allowed to cut up any more sponge heads though – think we used the quota for the summer.

1:47pm Camper: "Is London in England, or England in London?" Oh dear.

5:03pm Cara and me went and played tennis this afternoon. Well, tried to, we were useless. That bitch that runs the courts was definitely laughing at us. It was good fun for 15 minutes, and then we just felt stupid as some of the crafts kids had come to laugh at us through the wire too. Not good for the old ego.

Keakuki made me sit in bed with her after lunch. She's got this thick, black, unruly hair that I don't think she washes very often, it's a bit smelly and she has permanent bedhead. I'm learning to love the kids whatever though – all of them are a bit gross in some way. Keakuki has big, brown eyes and a wide frog-like mouth that's kind of scary. She always wears clothes that are too small or skimpy for her and thinking about her now I imagine her with flippers for feet – she pads along the hollow bunk floor slapping her feet down with every step, making far too much noise.

She took me through her school yearbook to show me her friends. Then she moved onto a photo album she had with 'model' pictures of her in. It was from one of those shoots where you turn up and they drape fabrics over you and plaster on the make-up. She said her dad had bought the makeover day for her and her mum to spend some time together. She was really excited and had the day off school to go and do it, but at the last minute her mum said she was too busy at work and so just dropped her off in the car to have it by herself. She was pretending like that was fine, but her parents just don't seem to care about her. She makes me so, so sad, what do you say to that?

8:17pm Argh, Jude is driving me nuts! She's so unnecessarily strict with the kids. She doesn't let them stay up reading at night – reading, for god's sake! They're good kids, she should give them some leeway. She's so snappy and mardy all the time, maybe camp is wearing her down – she looks absolutely knackered, but we all are. She's always nagging the kids to do this, do that. I'm genuinely worried about how I'm going to last another nine weeks with her. I want to put a pillow over my ears every time she talks and I actually have to count in my head to calm myself down.

9:16pm We got the list of campers for next session earlier. They won't arrive for another two weeks, but I think the head counselor wanted to warn us.
Rebecca: "Oh, shit."

Last year these campers were known around camp as the 'Mean Girls' – like the ones off the film. Apparently they're nasty, bitchy, cliquey, cruel hussies who, most importantly, were absolute shits to their counselors. Rebecca's friend looked after them – who hasn't returned this year – and she was always crying and saying how she just wanted to go home. Keakuki knew who they were straight away and was pretty much screeching the place down. She's staying for the whole summer, so she'll be in the bunk next session too. She was begging the head counselor to be allowed to change bunks. So, joy, *really* looking forward to next session now.

1:13am Just had another midnight staff meeting.
Earl: "I'm really proud of you all this year. We've recruited some excellent staff and you're all doing a great job, keep it up."

That was nice to hear – he even had a smile on his face. He gave the first Counselor of the Week award to one of the little girls' counselors. I wonder if I'll ever win it? Probs not.

It was so cold in there. We all sat snuggled up to one another in our big hoodies and hats. When it was time to leave we just looked at each other in despair – we'd all worked so hard to generate some body heat and we didn't fancy venturing out into the cold again.

Monday 20th June

7:57am Loudspeaker: "EEEEEEEEEEEEEEEEEEEEEEEVERYBODY UP, UP, UP, UP! IT'S TIME TO RIIISE AND SHIIINE..."
Oh god, not *every* day, surely?

9:14pm Night off and I'm off to the GC to celebrate. Found out today that Jude is being promoted to a head counselor because of her teaching experience. So woo, we'll be getting another bunk buddy in the next few days! I'm glad, working so closely with the same people day in and day out is really difficult. You see so much of each other and it's too easy to get on each other's nerves. And Jude was definitely getting on more than just my nerves.

I can see Cara coming towards my bunk; I swear she's not changed out of those Rockbear pyjama bottoms since she got them. She hasn't washed her hair either by the looks of it. When she can be bothered Cara looks really nice, but most of the time she slicks back her unwashed hair and rocks about the camp in her PJs. I think she gets it from the campers – a lot of them walk around in their pyjamas all day too. When I asked one of my campers about it she said she wears them to school sometimes too, how odd.

1:03am All the counselors are so horny here, it's hilarious. The boys walk around half naked checking everyone out and at night the GC turns into a pick-up bar. Literally, every way you turn couples are snogging each other's faces off. Not me tonight though. I hung out with Jamie, the journalist from video, and Danielle. We went for a crafty fag behind the shed on the golf course. We were messing around and taking loads of photos of each other. I'm getting a great tan already, making the bright jewellery I've made up at visual arts look wicked. Jamie said he'd help me make a video postcard in his studio. Basically you just use one of their video cameras to make a film of camp, as seen through your eyes, and then Jamie edits it down to three minutes and puts it on DVD for you to send home to dear old ma and pa. How cool is that? I'm going to make one next week, it'd be a nice thing to keep forever. Ah, I like Jamie he seems really cool and chilled and reminds me of my school friends. He's too short to be sexy, but I do like his big face.

A few of the American counselors have bought their cars here to use on their days off, but they're driving up to the GC in them because they can't be arsed with the hill. When the GC closes at around two they drive off to the next town along, Winkworth. There's this guy there who opens his massive house up for the counselors to go and get drunk and hang out in his pool. I haven't actually made it to his yet, sounds messy, and I'm normally too pissed by that time anyway.

Tuesday 21st June

11:25pm It was alternate day off today, so me, Emily, Danielle, gay Pete and around 20 other people on the alternate day staff went to this out-of-town shopping centre – it was brilliant! The camp driver, John, drove us and dropped us off for the day to pick us up later – it was only 45 minutes away. It's so good how Earl and Bud arrange stuff for us to do on days off, camp is really out in the sticks so we'd never get anywhere otherwise – there are no buses or anything. I still don't really even know where we are. Just that we're in New York State somewhere, about four hours from the City.

It was weird to be off camp, and a bit scary. I like having the security of Earl and Bud looking after us and knowing who and where everyone is – I feel safe. On camp all the decisions are made for us – even deciding what to have for lunch today was tough – and our day is timetabled to the last minute. Freedom feels weird.

On the way back we went to Walmart. I decided it would be a great idea to get on one of the motorised carts to take me around the store, but I couldn't drive it properly so I kept barging into things. Emily could hardly stand up she was laughing so much, tears were actually rolling down her face. She took a well funny picture of me red-faced and pissing myself laughing with the stern shop manager approaching behind.

Walmart manager: "These carts are for our less able customers only. Please get off it now, and put it back where you found it."

Oops.

Wednesday 22nd June

10:13pm The new counselors arrived today – there are loads of them!

I've been at camp for 17 days now and I love it. Imagine if I was at home, I'd have a job in an office and be getting pissed off with everyone and everything, dreaming of being abroad and working in the sunshine somewhere. Here I've gone days without thinking about home. There are so many things that make me happy here, mainly the people. Mine and Rebecca's new bunk buddy arrived earlier, Zoe. She's a model and has *the* best clothes. She's everything I imagine an Aussie girl should be: blonde, tanned, pretty and comes complete with a suitcase full of Billabong and Quiksilver surfwear. She's in the bed under mine – looks like I'm going to have to refine my getting in and out of bed skills so I don't kick that pretty little face of hers.

There's been so much gossip going around today, love it. Apparently two female counselors got caught doing rudies on the golf course at the GC and the owner is fuming, especially as he caught two guys at it under the terrace the other night. Hmmm, wonder who it was, there aren't that many gay guys on camp? Another one going around is that someone nicked a bottle of alcohol from the GC, and now they're threatening to close unless someone owns up. They must be well pissed off, but I bet that place makes more money in the three months we're here than in the whole of the rest of the year, you've got to take the rough with the smooth. We've got a meeting in a bit and we're all going to get *bollocked.*

1:13am Yep, we got bollocked. They told us if we didn't calm down they'd shut the GC for the rest of the summer. They tried to shame the person who stole the bottle of booze into owning up, as if that would happen. Earl was fuming, manic and after blood, the rage had turned his bulbous nose into a radiant beacon.

Thursday 23rd June

9:02am Every mealtime we have to queue outside the doors to get in the dining hall. It's *so* cold in the mornings and we're all there in pyjama bottoms and hoodies desperate to get in to the warm. The dewy grass tickling your feet through your flip-flops and the brisk morning air is not what you want first thing. Even when it's raining they only let you inside when all your bunk is there and you're being quiet and sensible. It's poo.

1:58pm Down at waterfront they have a massive inflatable iceberg and a huge trampoline, it's incredible. If the kids see a counselor there you can bet all they want to do is race you. Get down there at the wrong time though, and you'll be spending your whole free trying to boost the fat kids up. It's painful: they're pushing their trotters in your face while you're trying to stay afloat. The handles rip your hands and feet on the way up – it's worth it though to make it to the top. It must be about 30-foot high and looking around up there, you can see how remote the camp is in the valley. Trees surround us and you can't see another building for miles. Then you just take a deep breath, hold your nose and leap off the top screaming, feeling the rush of air over your body before you slap into the water.

The head lifeguard woman down there is *scary*. She struts around like Pammy off *Baywatch* with her high-leg swimsuit and long flowing locks. That's in her mind anyway. In reality she's about 60 and her ratty grey hair peeks out from under her cap. She's the one who gave me the filthy look when I got lost on the first day. She went mental at Cara and me yesterday for messing around on the diving board. She made us sit on the naughty step…

Cara: "But, we're…"

Lifeguard: "BE. QUIET."

Me: "Erm, excu…"

Lifeguard: "SIT DOWN AND SHUT UP."

Campers: "They're counselors!"

7:16pm My camper Keakuki breaks my heart. At meal times she rushes to the end of the table to scramble for any post from her parents, but there's never anything. The other girls get mail daily, but she hasn't had one thing since we started. She sits at dinner all sad and forlorn afterwards, with a look of hatred on her face as the other girls open their letters of love. I just want to put my arm around her, but I think she'd go crazy at me if I did thinking I was patronising her. She doesn't like to show weakness and puts on a tough exterior, but she sat there today looking like steam was about to blow from her ears.

11:18pm I've just been chatting to one of my campers, Joey. She absolutely loves it here and is a really talented singer, but she said this is her last year because her parents have told her she needs to concentrate on her studies. She's 13 and they want her to be a lawyer. She'd love to travel when she's older, but she says there's no chance of her parents ever letting her.

Joey: "They'd never let me get a job because they want me to concentrate on school, but there's no way they'd give me any money to go abroad either."

My parents haven't told me what to do since I was about 12 and they wouldn't. I know they coach and coax me around to their way of thinking, but they'd never give a definite instruction, they know it wouldn't work. I hate hearing about overly pushy parents. It's sad that gap years aren't big in America. I know there's some ridiculously high percentage of Americans that don't even own a passport – they need to learn that there's more to the world than just them.

Friday 24th June

2:02pm Cara and me went to try fencing today with my now ex-bunkmate Jude. We put on the big smelly outfits and had a bit of a play, but I'm not sure I really understand the point of it – or that it's even exercise. I got a bit hot just because of the suit, but apart from that it didn't seem hard. Ah well, was fun to give it a go. I could see Cara shudder as she took off the suit that all the kids had been sweating away in for the past two weeks. She hates anything dirty, gruesome or grotesque, she looked traumatised. I think Jude was a bit annoyed with us for not giving it a proper go. God I'm glad we don't have to work together in the bunk anymore. When she got promoted she also got her own double bunk just behind ours. It's cool, she's got her own bathroom and it's just her in there, she can even lock the door, wow.

Cara's so happy and confident when we teach together, but it makes me sad when I see her in her lesson with the other counselors. She's supposed to teach jewellery with Rebecca – which admittedly she has no interest in – but all she does is sweep the floor. She looked so forlorn earlier, like a starving street urchin trying to earn a dollar. Aww, she kept looking over at the kids too. I can just imagine Rebecca being really condescending to her and making her feel like that's all she could do. 'Webecca' can be really mean sometimes, and abrupt. I'm not sure she realises she's doing it, but she can make really cutting comments that hurt. She was saying something to me the other day in front of loads of people about how radio wasn't a real department, and that I had the shittest job on camp. I just let it go over my head; it didn't bother me that much and I don't want to fall out with her, but I'm starting to notice that she can actually be a real bitch.

11:43pm All the campers and staff went to a banquet today up at the dining hall. We got dressed up and the kitchen staff cooked loads of fancy food. They normally just hold a banquet at the end of the summer, but as this is the first year they've ever done four sessions rather than three, Earl wanted to celebrate the extra thousands of dollars lining his pockets.

We had amazing hors d'oeuvre in the upper camp's dining hall – king prawns, duck canapés, vol-au-vents – and then we gradually went through to the lower camp's dining hall to sit down and eat as normal. They made a massive cake with about an inch of frosting, decorated with the outline of one of the bunks and 'Rockbear 05' written across the top in even more frosting. Then we just went straight to Canteen and I had a bit of a dance with my campers – I felt like their embarrassing old aunty that was trying to 'get down with the kids', so I left them to it.

12:23am God I'm knackered, but I can't sleep. These girls are so funny when it's time for bed. They'll beg for a few minutes of torch time, so obviously I let them. They'll read or chat to the person in the next bed for about 10 minutes and then thank me, say goodnight, and turn their torches off. Awww, so sweet.

Saturday 25th June

12:15pm Teaching radio is rubbish. I thought it was all right at first, but all you do is stand there while the kids put CDs on. The hardest thing about it is trying to look busy when the other counselors go by as it's just near the staff room. The kids' musical repertoire stretches to *Hollaback Girl* by Gwen Stefani and that annoying *Don't Cha?* song, and that's about it. Those songs will forever remind me of camp. The kids usually get bored after about half an hour – if I'm with the cool kids we'll sit around chatting, when it's the annoying ones I end up spending the rest of the lesson telling them off and asking them not to play Frisbee with the CDs or write on the walls. The vending machines are opposite the radio shack so the kids normally buy some sort of sweets for me to enjoy, Keakuki's always good for that. None of them have turned up today

though, woohoo, another free. It's coming up to the end of the session so they're all busy with rehearsals for the plays. Rebecca's probably right, I might actually have one of the easiest jobs on camp. Although my social life here
is starting to take it out of me a bit, I'm exhausted.

6:56pm I've been chatting to my new bunkmate Zoe today. Every day I want to be wearing what she is. She's got this well cool Quiksilver khaki cap that would look so stupid on me, but with her bleached hair it looks wicked. She works at this clothes shop in Melbourne called Tea + Cake where she gets it all from. The kids loved her as soon as they saw her. I think I did too.

8:59pm My camper Keakuki gets so over-excited in the evenings, she's probably had too much pizza and ice cream. She runs around like a mad dog barging into the little kids and giving no thought to anyone else. She's giggling in the corners with the other girls about boys, but then it's always her friends that end up with them and she's by herself. When I'm DJing she storms into the booth and demands songs, jostling everyone out of the way because she knows me so she thinks she can. I let her because I feel bad for her, but it's not going to 'do her any favours', as my mum would say.

9:36pm Off to the GC – woohoo!

Sunday 26th June

12:40pm Oh dear. I seem to have got into a terrible habit of needing a poo at around 12 o'clock. All this boozing at the GC and fried chicken at lunch times is taking its toll. I'm meant to be teaching radio at noon and obviously I can't leave the kids too long without a co-counselor to cover. I'll get bollocked if I'm not there. I have to wait until I'm really desperate and then sneak off to the nearest toilet. The trouble is it's *very* near, as in about three metres away with the door facing the side of the radio shack. If any of the campers I was teaching came out of the radio shack to look for me, they'd be able to see me through the gap in the door. I have to make them pinky promise to stay in the shack so I don't get stage fright. Argh, it's so embarrassing, but it's one of those poos where you can't *not* go. Pooing in the bunk isn't all that anyway. It's so quiet in there in the day and there are always kids and counselors coming in and out. My preferred method of disposal is the individual portaloos near the woods – nice, private and peaceful and you don't get interrupted, so long as you find a quiet time to go.

1:52pm Rebecca and the younger girls' head counselor have made a chart where they write down the guys they've been with so far at camp and what 'base' they've got to. The results are feral. I think Rebecca might actually just be a slut.

4:48pm Rebecca, her best mate from last year Jo, and me have been so hungover today. Visual arts is definitely the best place to work when you've been drinking though. Everyone else has to stand out in the sun all day or work directly with their manager. The visual arts boss just hangs out in silkscreen all the time, which is in the shed down the hill, and she never checks on us. The three of us took it in turns to teach while the other two would sit in the jewellery stock cupboard scrunched up in a ball. I love this place.

Jo told me how much she likes the guy who runs lighting. He's all right and she's fun and I think he likes her too, but she's not one of the 'cool' kids on camp and he's superficial. He'll break her heart; he was flirting with me the other day right in front of her when it was obvious she likes him. She's so lovely and kind and definitely one of those counselors who puts the kids at the centre of whatever she does. Jo's kids love her; she's like a real big sister-type counselor. I imagine her and her kids have lots of heart to hearts, and she probably knows everything about them, whereas my kids and me just play and be silly – much more fun.

My campers are so easy to cope with compared with the stories I hear from the other counselors. They do everything I say and they're so loving and sweet. They just want to hang out together – they're not interested in boys or escaping the bunk in the middle of the night. I'm terrified for the arrival of the Mean Girls – how will I cope?

7:19pm I went down to the video department to see Jamie to try and make my video postcard earlier. The studio is filled with Macs, recording equipment and TVs, and the kids were sprawled out on mattresses on the floor working on their storyboards. He was sat in the middle of it all at the biggest screen and he swung round in his

chair when I came in.
Jamie: "Hey Lucy, what can I do for you?"

Gutted. He was too busy to help me today. It's nearly the end of the session so he has a backlog of kids' editing to get through so they can take them home.
Jamie: "Think about what you want to film though and we can go out together next week to do it. I'll give you some special attention." Haha, cue cheeky grin.

8:45pm I really hate watching magic. I hate that it's so tricky, and that it's *not* actually magic, it's just some crazy hand skills that I don't understand. We're watching yet another 'magic' show for evening activity tonight. The kids here are just learning and they're still all a bit shit. Eugh, I knew I'd hate it so I bought my diary along to write in instead.

I can see Earl out of the corner of my eye. His hairline's receding and the bit of fluff he does have is silver. He's got a huge snozzer and lips, and then the squintiest eyes ever. He's probably got hay fever – that could explain the big nose. He always wears the same camp-issue t-shirt and khaki slacks. I'd be scared of him if I was a kid, but they all seem to love him. He's always got a faintly amused look on his face that could go either way – psycho mad, or creepily kind. I've only said a few words to him when I've had to, he doesn't have much to do with visual arts. I have seen kids be well cheeky to him though. I guess he lets them get away with it – they're paying for his Florida mansion after all. During camp he lives in a big proper house on the grounds where only a few special counselors are invited each year. Doubt very much it will be me.

11:12pm Evening off tonight. I sat with gay Pete down at waterfront on one of the picnic benches under the trees. He's so funny, but just *so* up himself and judgmental – for some reason this makes me love him more, the cocky bastard. It also makes him great for a late night chat. Tonight he was launching into Rebecca and saying how she thinks she's just so cool with all her jewellery and 'boho' clothes.
Pete: "She makes out like she's this free-spirited traveller who doesn't care about the material things in life, but she's probably the most fake and superficial out of everyone.

Hmmm, could be true. I think I was a bit bedazzled by her at first and just thought she was really cool without actually really knowing her.
Pete: "Just the sight of her gets me angry. When she talks in that patronising way of hers I want to smack her."
Guess they're not going to be friends then.

As we were sat there I saw this guy who I hadn't seen before walking across the main path in the distance; he must be one of the new counselors. I could barely see him; just that he was very tall, my kind of stocky and walking like he was on a proper mission. It was weird – I was instantly attracted and I had to stop what I was saying and just watch him. Hmmm, I like.

Monday 27th June

6:57pm The arrival of the rest of the counselors the other day has seriously put our old-timer noses out of joint. When they're not swanning around camp like they own the place, they're up at visual arts using all the cool stuff that we weren't allowed to, to decorate their bunks ready for their kids in two days. I liked it before when we knew who was who, who's friends with who, and what was going on with everyone. They're changing everything.

I was chatting to one of them earlier, 'Pip'. She seemed pretty cool. We walked back to the bunks together and then realised she's in the bunk attached to mine – the one I was meant to be in. She's from Australia, but you wouldn't know it though to look at her. I always imagine all Aussies to have blonde, long, tousled hair and be super skinny and active, like Zoe. Pip looks like she's from England – she's a big girl and very pale, accentuated by her dark hair that she keeps swept back in a band. I hope she gets on alright with the South African and the American I thought I was sentenced to spending the summer with.

Speaking of Australians, my new bunkmate Zoe is absolutely useless. My love for her has quickly evaporated and she actually causes more work for Rebecca and me – her laziness and attitude is worse than the campers. I'm sure she'd be lots of fun if we didn't have to work together and we were just mates, but we're not, so she's really fucking me off.

11:16pm I've watched loads of end-of-first-session shows – *Blood Brothers, Ruthless, Rumours, Jesus Christ Superstar* – I was so proud of all the kids. I can't believe they put the shows together in just two weeks. The kids who I just see messing around in visual arts are actually really talented when they get on stage. I've seen a totally different side to them today.

When I got back to the bunk after the shows two of my new campers were in there a day early for the next session. I introduced myself, but they didn't really say much; just laid in their beds watching us with what I'm sure was pure disgust. They'd be the Mean Girls then. The doofus-like camper who loved me a bit too much at the start of camp tried to include them, but she was fighting a losing battle. I just left them to it. I wanted to concentrate on my first session girls for tonight, as it's their last sleep at camp. We played 'warm and fuzzies' at their request. Basically you say what you like most about each other, which is supposed to make you feel warm and fuzzy and you give each other a piece of wool as you say it. At the end of the game you weave the wool together to make a bracelet full of warm and fuzzy memories. There is *no way* I would've played this at their age. They were all so sweet though – saying that I was lots of fun and a few said that I was their favourite counselor, including Joey and Keakuki – and they were right, it did actually make me feel warm and fuzzy. I'm going to miss them!

Tuesday 28th June

10am Changeover day today and I'm gutted. It's amazing how close you can get to people in such a short space of time. I remember when the campers arrived and I was terrified – probably for the whole of the first week actually. I can't believe how well I've bonded with them in the end. The same goes for the counselors too. I haven't even known them a month and I genuinely feel like they've been my best friends forever.

Camper's mum (screeching from 10 metres away): "Hey Meegan, do you like my new fanny pack?"

Same camper's mum (now stood next to me): "You're from England? Do you know Prince William?"

Errrmmmm...

It was nice to see them with their parents, they were obviously happy to be together again, but you could tell they were kind of embarrassed too. It must feel weird going back home to normality after all the excitement of camp. Some of the girls won't see each other again until next year, that's if they come back, so they're quite sad to say bye to each other too. I wish I could go with them – the new girls scare me.

2:16pm Ooo, gossip: just found out the new woodwork counselor has been chucked out of camp already. He was so drunk when he came in from the GC last night he got in what he thought was his bed, but it actually belonged to a kid with Asperger's Syndrome. Apparently the kid was going wild screaming the place down.

Got chatting to the tall, stocky guy up at visual arts today. He's called Ben and he's working in painting and drawing. He's from Perth in Australia and is a graphic designer back at home. As he was talking I was just looking at his face: it's very structured with a clear jaw line and strong cheekbones. His kind, sparkly brown eyes balance out the harshness and his smile really lights up his face, although I do like his natural expression too. He's so unique looking, he fascinates me.

11:50pm Keakuki is the only one who's staying for the next session out of my bunk and the rest of the new girls arrived this afternoon. Oh. God. They are so different from my campers from last session. It's like I've travelled back seven years and I'm meeting myself aged 13. They came storming in moaning at their parents, or if their parents weren't there then they were moaning about them. As soon as they landed it was like a pink bomb had gone off in the bunk, exploding into an absolute shit tip. They've set up their pink bought-for-camp drawers, put out their pink bed linen, pinned up their pink fairy lights, unravelled their straighteners and now everyone's scrambling for space to put their endless clothes. Poor Keakuki is sinking in all the pink, and she is *not* happy. She was queen bee before, there's no way she will be with these girls. They all have so much stuff it's incredible. Their posters are up all over the bunk and smiling photos are around their beds. They've got Tiffany jewellery, Abercrombie and Fitch pyjamas and Chanel make up bags. I want the old girls back.

I can barely get a word in edgeways and they are *loud* – pretty sure there'll be no cringey silences with these girls. On first impressions, without needing the warnings from Rebecca and the head counselor, I'd say they were absolute bitches. They intimidate me, never mind Keakuki. They're moaning, squealing and talking hysterically over each other and the head counselor has already been in twice to try and get them to calm down. This is going to be a *long* three weeks.

Session Two

Wednesday 29th June

7:41am God, the toilets here are *so* feral. I don't even want to get out of bed to go, they're so disgusting and dirty. I can't face it first thing in the morning. The drains can't cope with the number of people using them and just keep blocking up. I'm sure the girls flush their tampons and pads down them when I've told them not to, they shouldn't block this much. When the girls need to go they're too lazy to use the plunger and so just piss on top of the overflow. By night time the toilets have stank out the bunk and there are poo particles swimming around on top where the drains are coming back up on themselves. It makes me heave. We have to get the handymen in to sort them out, eugh. Glad my bed is as far away from them as you can get. I don't know what the parents must've thought yesterday when they dropped the kids off.

1:15pm We had a six-minor day again today for auditions and tryouts. I got my new timetable – they've dropped creative writing, they must've worked out no one ever turned up. I would've thought all these angst-ridden teenagers would be into it, but apparently not. So, this is what I'll be doing for the next three weeks...

- 7:30 wake up
- 8:00 breakfast
- 9:30 rocketry minor
- 10:30 break and shower
- 10:45 crafts minor
- 11:45 break
- 12:00 radio minor
- 1:00 meet at the bunk
- 1:15 lunch
- 2:15 free
- 3:15 break
- 3:30 stained glass minor
- 4:30 break
- 4:45 leather major
- 5:45 break
- 6:00 dinner
- 7:00 rest hour

2:16pm The Mean Girls won't eat the food up at the dining hall. Apparently it's disgusting and unhealthy so they've bought crates of Cup Noodles – a bit like Pot Noodles, but with cheap packaging. I'm not sure why they think these are any better than the fatty food up there, but that's up to them. They sat down at lunch today with no food on their plates and then just brought a cup of boiling water back to the bunk to eat their noodles here. I hate eating in front of people if they're not, and they were staring at me too so I didn't feel comfortable eating much either. I'll be hungry for the rest of the day now. I hope they're not going to be like this for the whole session.

Campers aren't actually meant to bring food into the bunk, we're supposed to frisk them on the way in and give it to the front office, because of all the creatures about. These girls managed to get special permission for their Cup Noodles, but they're not supposed to have crisps and sweets. I'm going to bribe them with their supplies to keep their stash drawer a secret.

I'd got used to the old girls and had kind of settled into the idea that they were who I was going to be looking after for the summer. I think I forgot that I'd be getting new campers and I don't want them – it feels weird. They've obviously taken an instant dislike to me; I just don't know how to be around them. They're all so confident and assured; I'm scared of them and I'm being really quiet. For the first time in my life I feel really old. They all seem happy enough with each other – I'll leave it for a while until they come to me.

7:16pm Just been chatting to the camp director Bud about his favourite music – Billy Joel apparently. He's such a cool guy, Bud, not Billy Joel. He's got a kind and jolly face and thick, fluffy grey hair. He's a bit of a porker, but I think that makes him look friendlier. He's a fair man and the kids all like to chat to him. He knows his job like the back of his hand, he's been doing it for years and knows most of the kids by name – you can tell he tries his best with the counselors too. Although, I'd say he could be a pretty scary guy if you got on the wrong side of him, but I think you have to be like that when you work with children. To make the kids respect you they need to fear you a bit, or at the very least they need to see a flash of a dark side that could be unleashed any second. Bud does that well. He must get a huge buzz from his job, when the kids were telling me I was their favourite counselor the other night I loved it.

12:45am Oh my god, will these girls ever SHUT UP? I'm so desperate to just go to sleep, but the girls keep getting in and out of bed and stomping across the bunk. It goes quiet and then one of them starts giggling and sets the others off.

1:45am Rebecca's getting well pissed off, she just got out of bed and shouted at them. It made me jump.
Rebecca: "We've got to get up early and teach for six hours tomorrow – just shut UP, or I'll get Bud in here and he will not appreciate being woken up."

That seems to have done it, for now.

Thursday 30th June
10:36am Because the girls were up so late last night they were all exhausted this morning and wouldn't get out of bed, I had to ask them a million times. I really can't be arsed with this every morning. I can't go to sleep so late, I can barely keep my eyes open now and it's not even lunchtime. I sacrificed going to the GC last night for a good night's sleep, but instead I spent the night listening to the girls laughing and messing around. I'm not happy.

2:36pm Aww, the tall guy from visual arts, Ben, and me have quickly become best friends, except for the fact I really fancy him. He's so easy to talk to and when he smiles I just want to smile back. He's told me all about his life in Perth and what it's like living by so much wildlife and sea. He doesn't actually like water that much though. I've noticed that with quite a few Australians I've met here. I just assumed they all go for a morning surf before breakfast, think I've been watching too much *Home and Away*.

Ben's thing is art. He spends a lot of time in Perth's art galleries and he paints people he sees in the street – apparently he's quite well known around his area. He puts the paintings on show in exhibitions, which is pretty cool. He doesn't look like a typical scrawny, starving artist – although the proof is obviously in his pale sun-starved skin. He's very broad and his arms are huge, he says he doesn't do any exercise though. His big hands are sexy and he's so tall, about 6ft 5 – jackpot! He was wearing a white t-shirt today, with burgundy cords and flip flops, and ray-bans perched on his reddy/brown mop. He looks like someone from the film *Almost Famous.*

His nan brought him up as his dad was never around and his mum was always working. He looked to her for everything, bless him, he's definitely a 'sensitive type'. Hmmm, yeah, he's going to be good company for the summer for sure. Tim from rock shop keeps coming up to me in the canteen and trying to talk. He is really fit, but very dull. Ben seems really interesting; he had me intrigued when I saw him walking by the other night, and after talking to him I definitely want to get to know him better.

Every week each bunk gets a big blue drawstring bag and a white one, and the kids stuff them full of dark and light dirty washing to be sent away and done off-site. Rebecca said they always lose stuff so she doesn't use it, instead counselors can use the washing machines and dryers by the staff room, which is what I'm doing now. You have to sit with it to swap it over and buy your own powder and liquid, but it's better than getting your clothes mixed up with the smelly kids'. Although, I'm probably pretty smelly myself at the moment.

7:08pm Before every meal the campers have to meet back at their bunks before we can go up to the dining hall to eat. Even though they've all been to camp before and so know this, only about half of the Mean Girls were at the bunk before dinner. Rebecca had to go up to the dining hall and bring them back down before we could go up again as a bunk. This obviously pissed them all off, and me. Fuck, these girls are annoying. I swear they do it on purpose.

Rang mum earlier to tell her all about camp. It's difficult to know where to start. I told her about the video postcard I'm going to make with Jamie and she's very excited. I need to go and see him actually. He's probably busy at the moment with all the new kids – I'll give it a week. Sounds like everything is just the same old at home. I told her about the Mean Girls.
Mum: "Now you'll know what I've had to put up with all these years. Let this be a lesson in life for you Lucy."

8:16pm Cara is so, so funny with the kids – she should be Counselor of the Week for sure – they all think she's nuts. The kids love telling Cara how they're an eighth Irish, or at least their second cousin once removed is.

Camper: "Do you know Seamus O'Neill," or similar Irish sounding name.

Cara: "Ar yeah, went to school with him. Ah great guy."

They're so stupid they fully believe her – Americans definitely don't understand sarcasm.

Cara: "Ar fo god's sake, cop on!"

She always winds them up in our leather class too, telling them how we get the leather ourselves from the cows in the fields behind the mountains.

Cara: "I go out der wi' me big gun and shoot 'em down. Yous can see de bullet holes der."

The kids are open-mouthed fingering the natural, random holes in the big pieces of leather we have in awe.

Cara makes out like the kids annoy her and get in her way, but you can tell she genuinely loves them. She works really hard – her majors and minors are so much more fun than the rest of the counselors'. Watching her, I don't know how she ever held down a serious job though. She said she was a chef before camp, working long hours and even winning Pastry Chef of the Year 2002 in Ireland. I absolutely *cannot* imagine her paying attention for more than 10 minutes to bake something. She says she has ADHD, which doesn't surprise me. I'm actually jealous of all her energy.

I love teaching rocketry with her and we've got a really good group of kids this session. We have these packs for the kids with all the decoration and tubes and dynamite they need to build the rockets. All we have to do is show them how to do it. You basically just get the tube, hot glue the wings on, stick a few bits of decoration here and there – you can paint it if you like – and then attach the dynamite stick to it. Then in a week or so, and at the end of the session, we'll set them all off in the baseball field. The kids love the bangs and try to sneak more dynamite out of the other packets to make theirs go higher.

8:46pm Gay Pete and me went down to the water trampoline today in our free. It's *so* much fun. It's moored out in the lake and has inflatable sides with a bouncy centre so you can get a really good jump on and then dive straight into the water. I didn't enjoy the fact Pete was taking pictures though, all of which were completely hideous. It's not about bouncing up and down in a bikini with a load of scrawny 14-year-olds about – I looked like a whale in a goldfish pond.

9:23pm Zoe's so annoying. I liked it in first session when Jude was the really strict one who got the kids in line, Rebecca was second in command, and I was free to have fun with them. Since Jude's been promoted and moved out of the bunk we've all had to move up a step. Now Zoe is at the bottom having fun, booooo. She's so much worse than I was though; she acts just like a camper – actually worse than a camper – which encourages them to misbehave too. She has no control over the kids and doesn't seem to actually want any either. It's always:
Zoe: "Why do we have to do that? Who'd notice if we didn't clean the bunk? Who cares? Can't we just skip breakfast? Why do we have to get up so early?"

She's making it so hard for Rebecca and me to get the kids to do what we say. I can tell Rebecca's raging inside. She's gone really quiet like she's going to blow any second. If she's not frantically biting her nails, she's giving Zoe the filthiest looks she can muster – sometimes she even manages both simultaneously.

12:16am These new girls just don't do a thing I say, they're driving me crazy. I've had the head counselor in and Bud has threatened them with ETB 'Early To Bed' for the rest of the week, but they just don't care. I can't actually be bothered to try and get them to be quiet anymore. They don't listen. Arghhh!

Friday 1st July

9:21am I had to drag Keakuki out of the side door of the bunk in her bedsheet today, she just wouldn't get out of bed and we were late for breakfast. I dragged her across the bunk, down the steps and out onto the grass. She was laughing all the way, just squealing "Lucyyyy". She loved it, until she saw the Mean Girls looking on in disgust. I could tell they made her feel silly, and suddenly she hated me.

2:36pm I feel like Ben comes especially to seek me out at visual arts, not because he has anything in particular to say, but just because he wants to see me. He comes in my classes when he's meant to be teaching and pops his head round when I'm in the next department. I could be wrong, but I'd say he's into me. Ahhhh, too exciting!

In between lessons up at visual arts we have 'sunshine time' on the crazy golf course next to the studios. All the visual arts counselors go and sit in the sun and don't talk to the children when they come over – bit harsh, but funny and we're meant to have a five-minute break anyway. I sat with Ben on a different golf hole to everyone else, which is a big step in the world of camp counselor relationships. In some ways the counselors turn into teenagers again at camp, especially when it comes to the opposite sex. My heart lurches when I just sit next to him. I didn't feel like I could look at his face and in his eyes, it felt too much, like it was too intimate. I really had to force myself to look at him properly. Most of the time I was just staring down at his feet and legs – and he definitely has a delicious pair of those. His calf muscles are so taut; I really wanted to squeeze them. Too soon.

7:21pm Ben's bunk's table is only a few away from mine in the dining hall. He came over at dinnertime and all my girls just stopped talking and glared at him.
Ben: "Hey Lucy, are you going to the GC tonight?"

Ahh, so embarrassing in front of the Mean Girls. Inside my heart was pumping, but I managed to offer a casual 'yes'. He flashed his super sexy smile and subtly half-touched, half-stroked me on the back as he left to go back to his table. The girls had obviously got bored and were getting back to eating, but I was so happy. Zoe gave me a cheeky wink. I'll get to 'chat' to him properly tonight with no kids around, woohoo!

7:53pm We had a meeting today to discuss Independence Day as obviously they have huge celebrations here. All the counselors from the different countries are supposed to put together a skit to introduce their country to the kids – it could be anything, a song, dance, story – and you should get the kids to interact somehow.
Cocky know-it-all English counselor: "I've got it all in hand. It's a great idea, but I don't want it to get out so I'll tell you the night before. For now, just don't worry and make sure you have plenty of clothes with the Union Jack on."

Just because he's been coming to camp for a few years he thinks we should all listen to him. What's more annoying is that we did. Whatever he's got planned it better be good, there are more English counselors that any other nationality, so we have to be the best.

Saturday 2nd July

10:13am Eugh, day off and I'm on the way to Truhampton. Went to the GC last night and I'm not feeling well at all. Loads of people were out, so Emily and me decided it would be a great time to make the Official Camp Rockbear Porn Calendar 2005. We went round each person and made them pair up to do sexy poses for the camera. Emily found Ben and made him stand with his back against the bar while I was pressed against him with my leg bent around him and I turned to face the camera with my finger on my lip. My only defense is that I was drunk. After she'd taken the photo I turned back around and he kissed me, right on the lips. Toot, toot, what do you know, we ended up snogging for the next hour, haha!

Emily pretty much lost me for the night there, but before that she'd made Jamie and me sprawl over the table outside with me looking like I was enjoying him from behind. Everyone else who was there just piled on – that's going to be a well funny photo. Jamie's definitely fit, but Ben's better.

There were so many of us up at the GC the toilets were permanently rammed, so Cara and me decided to go on the golf course. We were midstream when the owner of the GC flicked on the floodlights and we were there with our trousers – well in her case pyjama bottoms – round our ankles. It was *so* embarrassing, everyone on the terrace was laughing at us.

After this Cara decided it would be a great idea to go joyriding in one of the golf carts. She 'drove' it down the steep GC hill and nearly knocked down some of our fellow counselors on their way back from the GC.

Endangered counselor 1: "Hey, who is that!?...."

Endangered counselor 2: "Oh, it's alright, it's just Cara and Lucy."

We were laughing so much it hurt. We got to the bottom then decided it'd probably be a good idea to do a Uey and put it back. So glad we did, we would have got an *absolute* bollocking from Earl, probably sent home actually. Actually, we still could if anyone dobs us in. Fuck.

On the way back from the GC to the staff room Pip, the cool girl from the bunk next door to mine, and me, decided to go and rob the ice cream room. It was funny, but actually really feral and gross at the same time, I'd hate to watch myself doing it. We were like animals desperate for food. We managed to open the doors enough to slip in and were pulling open all the big fridges to find the ice cream. We had the carton under one arm, and with the other hand we were scooping out the delicious ice cream into our mouths, pretty much sticking our fingers in one another's tub and feeding it to each other.

I walked in the staff room after the ice cream adventure and saw Cara sat on the sofa. I decided it'd be a great idea to jump on her. I misjudged, totally missed, and flew over the top of the sofa and cracked my head on the floor. I remember being in a lot of pain, it was a good job I was too drunk to really feel it.

Had such a good night. Ben and me ended up snogging in the staff room. Although, I'm shocked he even found me vaguely attractive. My t-shirt was covered in grass stains and ice cream, this blue mark I've now got on my head must have been a throbbing red one and I'm sure I had my half-smile-totally-pissed face on. Obviously that's what he's into because things got a bit heated on the staff room sofa. Mortified. I haven't felt this way about a boy for ages, my heart's flipping just thinking about him.

7:03pm Truhampton Shopping Mall was so dead considering it was a Saturday. Me, Emily and Pete had Subway for brekkers, it was perfect. Then we did a bit of shopping and went to Walmart – love that place. Left my mofo camera in there though – gutted! It had my international phone card in and more importantly, all the Camp Rockbear Porn Calendar photos. I went back, but someone had obviously already nabbed it. They literally would have been the greatest photos anyone had ever seen. Whoever picked up that camera will have a treat when they get home. I'm absolutely devastated. We had to come back early because the waterfront staff we were with had training, so gay Pete, Danielle and me are off to the GC for dinner. Hope they don't recognise me as the phantom golf course pisser, hopefully not without my accomplice in tow.

1amish Ooo, had a well tasty marinated grilled chicken sandwich at the GC – it was so good not to have to eat camp food. The GC was amazing, I've never seen it in the day and it's actually a really nice place. Pete was being very cute – he said he was so glad to have met us and that he was having the best time of his life. Then just as everything was lovely...
Me: "So how old were you when you realised you weren't normal?" What the fuck? I'm such an inbred. Everyone went silent for a minute then he laughed and told me to fuck off and we were all happy again. I'm such a twat sometimes. I don't know where these things come from.

Pete and me stayed on for a bit when everyone else got there, but we weren't drinking. I looked around and felt so happy: Emily and Cara were sat together pissing themselves laughing about something, Danielle was in the corner downing shots with another counselor from the climbing wall, Jo and Rebecca looked deep in conversation and Zoe and Pip were up dancing to *Land Down Under.* I love camp. I love all the people I've met here so much it makes me want to cry. These are all the kind of people who should be in my life.

Pete and me got a lift with the owner back to camp just after midnight as he was going that way, so I think I'm in the clear for the little piddle incident. So happy we didn't have to walk the ten minutes. We went to the dining hall for our coco pops fix and a cup of tea, then off to bed. Another perfect day!

Sunday 3rd July

9:15am I'm not even going to go into the trauma I have to go through every morning to get these princesses to sweep and mop the floor – it's too painful.

1:56pm Keakuki can be so loving and such good fun I really like her, but she makes me sad as I can tell her home life isn't the best. She likes it when I hug her, but I feel like the only reason she likes it is to show off to the other campers. If you hug her for a second too long or are genuinely concerned for her, further than the normal 'y'alright', she's horrible to you and tells you to get off. I'm sure it's some sort of weird defense mechanism she has. I feel like she doesn't want to enjoy the love too much or to cry. If she's not going crazy laughing and giggling, she's really down and looks so sad. There's no middle ground with her.

One of my new campers was saying earlier how she 'missed' her diamond watch. Apparently her dad is a famous diamond dealer and he wouldn't let her bring her jewellery to camp. Wow, she must have a lovely life.

2:40pm I was chatting to the little boys' general counselor earlier, he's fit.

Me: "So, anyone you're getting on with *extra well* at camp?"

Him: "No, not really. I'm definitely enjoying looking after the little kids though."

Me: "No one you've got your eye on?"

Him: "I don't see why people have come to camp just to spend their time getting with the other counselors. We're meant to be here for the kids."

Oh dear, awkward. Definitely not on the same wavelength there!

7:16pm I hate how the 'radio' shack where I have to teach 'DJing' is on the way to the staff room. There are always other counselors going by and I really feel like they look at me questioning my life's purpose here, and I'd have to agree. I don't do anything. I offer a meek smile and they carry on – on good days they'll come in and play with us – which is always fun. I don't know how the other guy does this all day, it's *so* boring, and lonely. It's not even a radio. I think towards the end of the sessions he lets them broadcast on a frequency through camp, but only those doing a major. Teaching radio is shit.

I saw Ben earlier and we were very coy around each other, it was funny.

Ben: "I had a really good time last night."

Me, with a smile: "Yeah, me too... it was err, fun."

Haha, I love all the embarrassment when you know you both know you like each other, but everything is just slightly awkward. It gives me a rush.

12.22am Oh god, the girls are going crazy. I've just got back from the midnight staff meeting expecting them all to be asleep, but they were wandering around in their pyjamas saying some girl has broken into camp and is after them. Apparently Earl wouldn't let the girl come back this year because she slit her wrists while she was here last year, and now she's escaped her care home and the Mean Girls reckon she's after them. What the fuck? These kids are crazy. Now they're just frightening each other and spurring each other on. Has this really happened? How can they be so worked up if it's not true, but how can it be true? I very much doubt some 13-year-old has managed to break out of a mental home and get to outback New York by herself. Argh, I can't be bothered with this. I'm debating whether to move to a younger bunk.

Earl was raging at the staff meeting because from the start of camp he's said that under no circumstances is peanut butter to be allowed on the campgrounds. Some kids have serious allergies to it and he says it's not worth it. They have some fake stuff up at the dining hall and when we do our food check at the start of each session we're supposed to do an extra vigorous check for peanut butter. One of the boy campers this session has managed to get it into camp and was found dealing a black market in it up at the dining hall. Earl's enraged.

He's also angry that someone stole the inkpot made of icing that was on the cake we had for the first session banquet. It's gone from the kitchen and he wanted to keep it and use it again for the cake in the fourth session. Someone's going to be in big trouble judging by the shade of his face.

1:04am There's this five-foot monster in my bunk, known to her parents as Britney. She's such a little bitch it's incredible. She's the ringleader in all this crazy girl talk: as soon as the other campers are peaceful she'll start them up again by saying she just saw the girl out the window again, or some other bullshit. I bet she's pure evil to the younger kids at school. I guess she has to be feisty to stand up for herself, but she just takes it to a whole other level. She's so small, so she's years behind the other girls in development, but is obsessed with boobs. She wants what the other girls have, but bullies them for it at the same time. Everything she says is loaded with bitchiness and she picks up on any self-doubts and rips them apart. She's actually really popular though – I'm putting this down to the fact she came in a big group of girls so she's always got them behind her. She's quite scary to watch – I wonder what she'll be like when she grows up? Argh, wish they'd shut up. I want to go to sleep.

1:35am They've finally calmed down and it sounds like Britney's snoring a little. She has to wear this head brace for her teeth at night – looks very painful, and a little bit funny. Right, sleep time, thank god.

Monday 4th July – Independence Day!

2:23pm Some of the British counselors started the day off singing *God Save the Queen* on the loudspeaker across camp – I couldn't be bothered to get up early enough. The camp was covered in England flags; they were chalked on the floor, hung outside the bunks and pinned to every notice board. Apparently it's traditional for all the kids to dowse the British counselors with shaving foam and before I'd even made it to breakfast I'd been sprayed about five times.

Zoe got some of the kids she teaches at drama to water bomb me when I got out of the dining hall after breakfast; I noticed how she didn't get Rebecca though. I like to think this is because I'm fun and Rebecca's scarily mardy, not because they all hate me. This made me five minutes late for rocketry. When I got there Cara had given all the kids cups and bottles and she had a bucket of water – they drenched me when I walked in. Hearing the kids' hysterical laughter made it ok, but I need to think of something good to get Cara back.

After rocketry all the kids were telling Ben to chuck me in the lake. I can't believe how much abuse I've already had today. I was pleading with him not to, but obviously in a pathetic girly way. I wasn't really that bothered. He scooped me up and chucked me over his shoulder in a fireman's lift and all the kids were cheering. He started off well, but after about two minutes I think he was regretting launching my 10-stone weight on his back. The kids were all egging him on to throw me in so he couldn't back down now. I could feel him buckle under me, especially as I kept slapping him on the back to let me go, but he stayed strong. I loved it really, but I felt like I had to do that whole flirty thing girls do when they like a guy. Haha, I'm smitten. He smelt so good and I gave his bum a cheeky squeeze when the kids weren't looking. I think he was trying to hold his breath to give him the extra oomph to get through the 5-minute walk down to waterfront. In the end he gave up and pretended to be nice by dropping me on the sand just a few metres short of the lake. Oh dear, must stop eating all those chicken wings at lunch times. I was laughing and ran back to visual arts with the kids, but turned around to see him bent double with his hands splayed on the picnic table breathing heavily.

7:07pm The horsey lot dyed two of the horses blue from top to tail. They looked amazing, like magical creatures from a fantasy film. I don't know what they've done with them; they're probably hiding them from Earl. He'll go mental if he sees them.

After lunch Cara pulled the same trick as she did in rocketry and got all the stained glass kids to throw water at me when I arrived. A few of my favourites looked really hesitant to chuck it at me, which made me love them even more. The Mean Girls were walking past as the kids drenched me: unimpressed was not the word. It's like they think they're too cool to have fun. They rolled their eyes and carried on – like they judged me unworthy. They're the ones missing out though, the stained glass kids were pretty much on the floor laughing, bless them.

Found out it was Zoe who stole the icing inkpot. Haha, legend. I wouldn't tell Rebecca that if I was her though, those two are *not* getting on.

I really don't know what last night was about with the girls. They seem convinced that they saw this girl on camp – but the head counselor has no idea what they're talking about either. Strange children.

11:16pm After dinner we had the Independence Day celebrations. Every country did a sketch to do with their country; England's was *so* embarrassingly shite. That douche guy that said he had a great idea dressed up in a Darth Vader outfit – that was it! We all stood around him tunelessly singing *Three Lions*, it was pure cringe. The Kiwis did the Hakka, the Scots gave them some native words and the Aussies taught them to sing *Land Down Under*.

Then we went to the Kennedy Theatre to watch the camp orchestra play some classic American tunes. We all stood up to sing *Star-Spangled Banner* with our hands on our hearts looking toward the flag – hilarious. There was even a sheet under the flag in case it came unhooked and fell on the floor.

After that Bud put on the most amazing firework display I've ever seen. The whizzes and bangs went on for ages and they spelt out 'Camp Rockbear' in fire. I also had one of *the* most intense moments of my life. I got there and I was desperately trying to find Ben. I wanted to check he was all right from carrying me earlier and because I wanted to see him, obviously. I just feel better when he's around. Anyway, I couldn't see him anywhere without making it too obvious by asking around, so I gave up and just stood leaning against the supports in the canteen watching the fireworks. I felt him come up behind me and my heart literally skipped – I swear I can sense when he's around – cheesy, but true. I'll probably be sick when I read this diary back in the future. So him and me were stood there looking at each other – we obviously can't touch or kiss or anything because of all the kids around – then he touched my arm and whispered in my ear.

Ben: "I wish you were coming to the GC tonight. You sure you can't get it off?"

Argh! There is just so much sexual tension between us that we can't do anything about. We were surrounded by kids and counselors, which made it all the more exciting and charged – it's always more interesting when you shouldn't be doing whatever you're doing. We couldn't talk properly because we were supposed to be watching the kids and Earl would go crazy if he saw us stood around the edge chatting while fireworks were exploding around us. God, I really fancy him! I was so desperate for him to put his arm around me, or kiss me, or something! It was more than intense. Then the fireworks stopped, the music started and everyone on duty – me – had to get back to their bunks. I squeezed his bum and stroked his arm as I passed and he turned and smiled cheekily. Argh, hot! I can't stop thinking about it – wish I was up at the GC!

12:56am There are so many kids in my bunk this session; I'm finding it really hard to get to know them. I need to make friends with the leader and then get through to them that way. Hmmm, who's the leader? Shit, they've been here a week and I still don't know all their names. It's probably Britney. I feel like they all hate me. In some ways it's like being at school again, I'm trying to get in with the cool crew, except I don't actually want to get in with them, I just want them to do as I say. I sat with two of them last night and we actually had good fun and a nice chat, it's just hard when there's a wall of 12 of them. I don't like having to be so nasty and bossy to them, but I have to be because they're so rude and lazy.

Hmmm, wonder what Ben's doing up at the GC?

Tuesday 5th July

2:23pm So much has happened, I don't know where to start. Video Jamie, Anna from circus and one of the new counselors Leith, were in a car accident last night. Jamie and Anna are dead and Leith's in hospital with a broken neck. It's been absolutely, unbelievably awful.

Today should have been a lazy day. All the other counselors were meant to be out, but this morning there were no buses to take them, which everyone thought was odd, but no one knew why. Earl and Bud weren't at breakfast, but I didn't think too much of it at the time. Then at around ten Earl announced over the loudspeaker that all the campers and counselors were to come immediately to an assembly at the Kennedy Theatre. I rounded up the kids and we went over – you could tell straight away something wasn't right. All the head counselors, Earl and Bud were stood with stern, blank faces. It didn't take long for the kids to shut up this time.

Earl: "There was a car accident last night."

Just in that one sentence he had to keep stopping to catch his breath and bite his lip. He paused. Some of the kids had started whimpering and crying already.

Earl: "Anna and Jamie have died... Leith is in intensive care."

He had to stop again. More kids were crying as they took in the news. You could see the counselors were trying to hold it together too.

Earl: "They were driving away from camp and there was a deer in the road. They swerved to avoid it... and hit a tree."

He stopped, for an uncomfortably long time.

Earl: "I know a lot of you will be very upset. For the rest of the day a few of the shops will be running, but take your time to think about Anna, Jamie and Leith."

By now a few of the kids were wailing. Bud had stepped up to stand next to Earl as he was obviously struggling.

Bud: "Talk to your counselors as much as you need – stay here if you want – and remember we're here to help you."

The meeting ended and Earl went straight back to his office, but the head counselors and Bud stayed behind. How could this happen at camp?

I took my campers back to the bunk and a few of them got in bed crying while others just lay staring at the ceiling. I didn't really know how to react or what we were supposed to do.

I didn't actually even know who Anna was, but apparently she'd been coming to camp for years as a camper and this was her first year as a counselor. The Mean Girls knew her well, so were really upset. I didn't know Leith either. I tried to remember him standing up in front of everyone at the Independence Day celebrations as he did the skit for Scotland, but I can't.

But I did know Jamie, and I can't believe he's gone. That's it – I'll never see him again. It's crazy. He was so lovely and nice and from what I knew of him, such an amazing person. I only saw him yesterday, and now he's dead. How can that happen?

8:12pm Rebecca said someone told her that Jamie had actually been drink driving and speeding and that the deer story is a cover up for the kids. She said she saw them speed into the camp at about midnight, do a 180, and go out again too. Other people are saying that he was racing someone else; I guess we'll never know.

I knew them taking their cars to the GC and round the town was a bad idea. Being at camp with all the other counselors – even though I've never even spoke to some of them – you just feel a strong allegiance to each other. It's such an intense situation that the other counselors start to feel like family. You kind of feel responsible for each other's welfare, like you should've been looking after each other. I feel guilty for some reason.

I imagine them being hyper up at the GC and deciding it was a great idea to go for a spin to Winkworth, Jamie was probably showing off to Anna by jolting the steering wheel and going too fast. What the hell was he thinking? There were loads of people at the GC last night and usually about ten or so people go on to the guys house along the road for an after party, but last night it was just Jamie, Anna and Leith who went. If only there had been another lot of counselors going – they would have got there and when Jamie's car didn't arrive they would have raised the alarm. I feel so, so sorry for their families, they must be in total shock. You don't say bye to your child leaving for summer camp and not expect to see them again.

9:15pm I've just seen Jamie's camp girlfriend at the front office. She feels so guilty for not being there and not stopping him, she's distraught. I can't believe this. Some of the kids haven't stopped crying, while I think others who didn't really know them feel a bit weird as they don't really know what to do with themselves.

11:16pm It's pissed it down all day today. Everything about camp is grey and tragic. I rang mum and as soon as I heard her voice I started crying; I couldn't get my words out. This wasn't supposed to happen at camp. I had to sneak out to the portaloo earlier to cry as I didn't want the kids to see me upset.

I've sat down with each of my campers individually to talk as some of them have known Anna all their camp lives. Rebecca is devastated – she was good friends with Anna from last year – so I just told her to look after herself and I'd help the kids. Although she's now been face down in bed all day and I kind of need her to help.

I think a few people are just caught up in the drama of it all. I'm sure some of them are not actually upset about what's happened, but just upset about the mood on camp. Zoe is one prime example. She's been even more annoying than usual. After we came back from the Kennedy Theatre and Rebecca was crying in bed, I was trying to calm 12 dramatic teenagers down and she just fucked off to Winkworth for a restaurant dinner with Pip. Obviously when she got back I asked her where the hell she'd been:
Zoe: "It's just so depressing on camp, I couldn't hang around."

What the fuck? Jamie had been filming a show for her so she's decided he was her best friend and that for some reason she's more important than all the other kids and counselors. She's apparently the one who deserved to get out of camp. Zoe hasn't helped with the kids one bit – she never even came to dinner with us when she got back. If Earl found out he'd go crazy. How can she be so selfish today? I'm pissed off at Pip too. These past few days I've thought she was wicked, but at times like these you show your true colours. Why do they think they can get off camp? Everyone's in the same boat, we should be helping each other. Zoe's actually just used the death of two people as a chance to bunk off. God, she's just *so* shite, she's really outdone herself this time with her purely selfish actions. I'm angry, but I need to stop thinking about her and concentrate on what's important.

On a different note, Ben has been absolutely amazing today, so supportive and such a great listener. When something like this happens you really assess what's important to you, and he is. I've only known him a week, but I really like him. A lot.

Wednesday 6th July

8:16am I couldn't sleep last night. I just kept thinking about Jamie and Anna's last minutes. I wonder how long they knew they were in danger? Like, whether they were just looking the other way and it was a split second until they crashed into the tree, or whether they were all screaming as they slid into it. I'll never know. Whether it was just for a second or a minute it must have been so scary. I can't imagine how it feels to know that's the end.

2:18pm The kids have calmed down a bit. The whole situation has bought me closer to them as they've just needed someone to talk to, but this definitely isn't how I wanted it to happen. They're even affectionate with me now – which I'm finding a bit odd.

I spoke to Cara about it earlier. She's upset, but not obviously and I think she's a bit confused about why people who didn't even know them are crying still. I guess when you look at it like that you could side with her, but I'm genuinely devastated. Pete is on her side, he's just carrying on as normal. I can't believe it's only been a month since we arrived at camp, I feel like a totally different person, especially now this has happened.

2amish Night off tonight so Danielle, Emily, driver John, and me, went to Winkworth for a drink. We slowly drove past the spot where Jamie and Anna died – it was awful. Judging by the tyre swerve marks on the road John reckons Jamie was speeding at over 90mph down the country roads, with Anna and Leith both on the passenger side. John stopped and we walked around looking at the horrific scene. It was so overwhelming and horrendous to think that this was the exact spot where they'd died. Right there where I was standing, that was the end of them. I couldn't stop crying, not just with tears, but my whole body was shaking. After the past day of soothing the kids the grief was catching up with me. Anna and Jamie dying so pointlessly and stupidly like that seems ridiculous. What a waste of two lives, just because they were drunk and thought a joyride would be fun.

It wasn't really helping anyone being there; in fact we were all getting worse, so John made us get back in the car and drove us on to Winkworth. We couldn't speak for the whole journey; we were just whimpering and staring out of the window.

We got to the bar and it was fun, at first. We'd managed to stop crying and John was buying us drinks, but then it felt wrong to be having fun. How could we be enjoying ourselves drinking in a bar when this is part of what killed Jamie and Anna? They'll never be here again, and that feels insane. It seems odd and uncaring to even try to get back to the way it was before. The safe bubble around camp that I'd taken for granted has burst – I really can't cope with, or understand, death. One of my best friends died when I was 13 and it still upsets me to think about.

We talked about how sound Jamie was, and how he would've loved to have been out with us. We'd had a few drinks by this point so we started getting even more emotional. It's so hard to deal with this massive event in such an odd and enclosed environment when none of us have a minute to think by ourselves. Camp is an emotional place. Everything that happens here seems at least five times worse than it would be in the real world. You're closer to people here after a week than you ever normally could be.

We were all sat crying at the bar and getting some funny looks from the locals so we left. We went back via the crash site. We'd bought a US flag and flowers and placed them on the exact spot. After one last look and cry we drove to have a drink with the guy who opens his house down the road. I was absolutely exhausted and just fell asleep on a bench as soon as I got there. I don't think it was much fun as the next minute they were shaking me to wake me up to come home.

When we got back I went to the staff room to see if there were any fun people about – when I say fun, I mean Ben – but there wasn't. He was so amazing to me yesterday I just wanted to be with him.

Thursday 7th July

8:26am Woke up this morning to hear there'd been a terrorist attack in London. I don't know exactly what's happened, all we've heard is that a bomb went off on the Underground and people have died. I was so scared when I found out – I ran across camp and phoned dad from the front office straight away. I felt sick at the thought he might be there – he wasn't answering his phone. I managed to get through to Nan who said he wasn't actually even in London, thank god. It was a slight overreaction on my part there, but you just think the worst when you're so far away from home and everything seems to be going wrong around you.

9:10am The staff room was packed over breakfast – all the English counselors were glued to the TV. Bud is being such a cock about it though. He called a meeting on the tennis courts after he realised all the English counselors were missing from breakfast.
Bud: "You should think yourselves lucky more people haven't died. Almost 3,000 died in the World Trade Centre attacks."

Loads of people here are from London, or know Londoners, so it's a pretty fucking insensitive thing to say. That's probably the first thing Bud's done that's made me not like him. Up until now I thought he was such a cool guy. He told us to get back to work. It's all made me realise how remote we are – anything could happen in the outside world and we just wouldn't know about it. In fact, I don't actually know anything else that's been in the news this last month.

9:30am Aww, the head counselor just told us we've won Super Clean Up. While we were in the staff room the campers had really blitzed the bunk and made it neat and tidy with everything in its place. That was so sweet of them; I'm shocked. Maybe they're not so bad after all. We'll get taken out for pizza tonight as a reward now. Mmmm, just what I need to cheer me up a bit.

2:26pm I spent my radio minor with Ben as no kids turned up, again. We lay on the sofa in the staff room together just chatting. He told me there's a 'spiritual gift' within his family and that he's been able to hear the dead speaking before.
Ben: "I have a strong connection with auras and I can see people in colours."
Me (in my head): "What the fuck?"

It's a really big thing for him and he said how annoying it is when he tells people and they expect some sort of evidence – just as I was about to ask him for some sort of evidence.
Ben: "It'll come naturally as we get to know each other more."

Now there's a loaded comment, I like. I knew he was a sensitive, feels-everything-more-than-most kind of guy. He wouldn't really go into it that much, but he said that back home his sister runs clairvoyancy nights where she'll talk to dead relatives for people. I'm not sure what my feelings are about all that. I don't really see how it can be true, but then some people live their lives by the stars and all that and find comfort in spirituality, so I guess there's got to be some truth in it somewhere.

We lay there non-stop talking for the hour, no kisses though – for some reason we've both gone really shy over the last few days. He feels like a high school boyfriend where we're too nervous to make the first move, but you can both feel you want to. I'll try and find him for a little kissy tonight when we get back from our pizza session.

Two of my campers are still saying they want to go home. Anna's death has really got to them and Rebecca moping about the bunk isn't helping the mood. All her family and friends are fine in London, but I guess she's still shaken up. It was an explosion on a bus near Russell Square, which is apparently just up the road from her flat. I guess she's freaked out that she could have been there and a lot of her friends would've been around the area. I totally understand the campers wanting to leave – I can't believe these kids come for so long without seeing their parents – three weeks is a long time at 13 years old.

1:30am We never went for pizza for Super Clean Up. Instead, Earl decided to have a midnight staff meeting and give us all an absolute bollocking about Jamie and Anna. What a complete knobhead.
Earl: "What the hell do you think you're all doing?"

He shouted at us then went silent. Some of the counselors were starting to cry.
Earl: "Tears are useless now."

He said it had been the worst day of his life. He was a personal friend of Anna's parents as she'd been coming for 12 years and to have to ring them and say that their daughter had died was the worst thing he'd ever had to do.
Earl, raging now: "Do you think you're all invincible?"

He just managed to stop himself from crying. He's closed the GC and no one is to go off camp until he says. He made his point, but he's not really shouting at the right people. We weren't the drunken people that got in a car in the middle of the night and went speeding. He's had a horrific time, but there was no need to shout at us all like that, we've had a hard time too. I don't think he needs to worry that it will happen again.

Friday 8th July

9:16am At breakfast the girls were taking the piss out of my campers from last session for the 'warm and fuzzies' game they played on the last night. They were actually being pretty funny and did make me laugh. Although I felt like a traitor, the girls from last session were so innocent and lovely. You wouldn't believe these girls were the same age – 13 really doesn't mean anything. Keakuki's mature in her body but not in her mind, then there's the little bitch Britney, well judging by what she talks about she'd be 18, but when you see her she looks more like eight.

Keakuki hates these new girls. She must be one of the odd ones at school – she's loud, scruffy and overweight – pretty much like I was. Although, I like to think I was more popular. Maybe that's why I feel some affinity to her when the other campers moan and bitch about her. These new girls are the cool, rich girls that all the boys like. They probably shit all over girls like Keakuki at school. I can see there's just no way they'll get on. Keakuki's asked if she can move bunks and I think it's for the best. She just doesn't fit in, and won't, and there's no point forcing it as they're only here for a few weeks. I can always see the other girls sniggering and bitching about Keakuki behind her back, so can she, and it's really sad.

It's been four days now since Jamie and Anna died and people have stopped crying sporadically, but you can definitely feel the sadness over camp. I can't imagine it ever feeling completely normal again.

The Scottish girl I sat next to on the bus on the way here is leaving tomorrow. She was really upset about Jamie, and couldn't believe the way they treated everyone over the London attacks so she's going. She said last night's telling off was the final straw. She asked to leave and they told her it would have to be tomorrow, and no later – I guess they don't want her here with a negative attitude if she doesn't want to be here. It seems so drastic. It has been horrible lately, but going home early is a rubbish thing to do, and she won't get paid. In fact, I think you have to pay some money to the agency if there's no valid reason to not fulfill your contract. I don't think the fact they're being a bit shit will cut it.

12:23pm Saw Ben on my way to visual arts earlier. We spotted each other, looked both ways, and then ducked behind the costume shop for a quick snog – delightful.

6.30pm God the Polish staff do not get off the phones. Argh! I've skived off dinner so I can talk to my parents properly, but they're always in the phone boxes jabbering away. It's so annoying – there are only two phones between all the counselors so sometimes you can give up your whole hour break trying to phone home and still not get to do it. The booths are really small, sweaty and stink of wet wood, eugh. Woo, at last, my turn.

11:16pm The 10-13-year-olds' head counselor is a weird one. She and Rebecca are really good friends so she's always hanging around our bunk. I think she's from Bristol or something, not that that matters. She's one of those people who doesn't look at your face properly when she's talking to you, like there's something massively important going on behind you that she doesn't want to miss. She's a little thing, but a massive chav with scary drawn on eyebrows that rise up too high and her hair is slicked back as tight as it will go. She seems such a random choice for a head counselor, she's not approachable at all, and she's definitely not the friendliest person in the world. I can't imagine her sorting out the kids' problems and being understanding when they're sad. I wouldn't want to go to her with my issues, that's for sure.

Our head counselor is a good choice, but I don't think she likes me much. I swear whenever I'm not being as good a counselor as I should be – having a cheeky nap, or chatting to the other counselors instead of the kids – she's always there. She's never there when the campers are telling me how much they love me, or we're having in-depth chats or I'm doing cool stuff with them. She seems to find the whole camp thing pretty funny, which is a good attitude to have. She just laughs at everything and always finds in favour of the counselors when the kids are being shitty. The other day evil Britney was trying to get us in trouble with her. She strutted back to us and was like, "The head counselor wants to see you". Then our head counselor told us what Britney had said and that she knew it was lies. We just ended up having a chat while poor little Britney thought we were getting a telling off. Haha, bitch.

Saturday 9th July

2:36pm Meal times are really hard work with these girls. Everyone has to be sat upright and quiet before your table gets to go up and choose dinner. They *never* sit quietly: cue 20 minutes of me telling them off and asking them to calm down. They know Earl will eventually have to let us go eat, so they don't bother shutting up. I'd be up for just sitting talking until we're called, but if Earl sees me doing that I'll get a bollocking so I have to just pointlessly moan at them until we're the last ones left and Earl wants to eat his own dinner so lets us just go up anyway. Bud's empty threats of ETB never work; the girls know he won't go through with it. He should just enforce it one day without taking it back for some credibility.

Keakuki moves to another bunk today. I'll be sad to see her go, I feel like we've become best mates in the bunk and I like hanging out with her. I'll still see her around camp though; she's here for the *whole* summer.

All the other counselors seem so negative about camp at the moment, I need them to be happier and enjoy it more so that it rubs off on me. It's been so shit this past week with everything; I'm debating going home it's that shit. I've been here for five weeks now and I'm really not enjoying looking after these campers; they're *such* hard work and literally won't do anything I say even after asking a million times. I'm going to go crazy at them soon. I want to change to a younger bunk just to get away. Zoe's got a good way of dealing with them when they won't listen, she just sings. She sings non-stop in a really annoying nasally way until they do as she says because they just want her to shut up. Woah there, Zoe in rare 'doing her job' moment, glad I recorded that, I can't imagine it'll happen again.

7:14pm I feel so shit about everything at the moment. I keep thinking about the Scottish girl who left. I bet she'll be all tucked up at home now, in the safety of her home and family. I don't know if I could actually leave, even if I wanted to. I'd be so embarrassed to go home and not see it out after all the fuss I made about coming here all this time. I'm seriously thinking about it though – these kids are a nightmare, Rebecca and Zoe are doing my head in and I'm just so tired – everyone's so miserable, it's shit.

8:59pm Britney's got this little acne-ridden friend who's really funny and obviously very rich. They've made 'the pact' that they'll get married to each other if neither of them have a partner at 30, although I'm pretty sure he's gay. He minces around with his handbag and pouts permanently for his imaginary paparazzi. I'd say about 80 per cent of the boys here are probably gay. I guess it is a performing arts camp. I sat with him and Britney on the two armchairs she bought to camp especially, earlier. We were out on the grassy area in front of the bunk and I was on one and those two were on the other. They kept doing filthy sex positions and asking me if they were doing them right. I can't believe she actually brought two proper bright pink armchairs with her; I bet she leaves them behind as well.

I'm a bit jealous of how much the kids love Zoe. Although, they have admitted they only like her so much because she's shit and lets them do what they want. She is cool, and I'd definitely love her if I was a camper, but she just doesn't do *any* work. She gets away with it and is effortlessly the favourite; it's not fair. The campers love playing with her clothes, she's got so much cool stuff with her – fun handbags, belts, tops, jewellery – loads of stuff that makes her look instantly cooler. Oh god, I've just realised, I'm probably the dorkiest of us three in my ¾ khaki trousers, Birkenstocks, and surf t-shirts. Hmmm, I wonder if my new best friend Zoe will let me borrow some cool things? Not if she ever reads this diary, that's for sure.

Sunday 10th July

12:06pm We went to a bar in Winkworth last night seeing as the GC is still closed – it was so good. I felt carefree and everyone was crazy drunk. It was just what everyone needed to relax and chill out after the last week. I'd heard the locals all thought we were crazy before, now they definitely will. Pip and me had a little smooch; Zoe wasn't having any of the free love though. I had a great drunken chat with Ben round the back of the bar. We talked about when we first saw each other and how we were both immediately attracted. As soon as he saw me he couldn't stop thinking about me. Obviously this led to an epic snogging session and we barely spoke to anyone else for the evening. He kept buying me drinks and I ended up absolutely steaming drunk. I was so comatose in the car on the way back I didn't even realise they'd all been to McDonalds for an hour, until we got back to camp and I saw all the boxes. Oops.

Ben and me mooched around camp for a bit to try and get rid of the smell of booze before going back to sleep in the bunk. Instead we ended up in the staff room. We thought no one else was in there and ended up getting frisky out the back in the washroom, on top of a washing machine. It was really fun at the time, but again I'm absolutely mortified. What if someone saw us? Anyone could've just been walking past or even come in and we probably didn't notice. Fuck, I hope no one saw us. Imagine if a camper did? We'd be chucked off camp straight away. I'm sure they wouldn't – that would mean them being out of their bunk at 5am – which they wouldn't be. I'm so paranoid. At the same time I can't wait for the next 'wash night' though, only got about two hour's sleep. Tee hee!

1:53pm I swear you lose track of the days here until Sunday comes around and you realise there's no post. We've only got one week left of this session, and then we'll be halfway through the summer. It's going so fast.

After the iPod paintings we did in the first session there was still one wall left that we randomly didn't use. Ben's done a painting of what looks like him, but with wings on a cloudy background, and written a dedication to Jamie and Anna at the bottom. It looks really good, although at the same time I find it a bit cringe. He's making this grand gesture to some people he didn't even know – and made himself the face of it. Just a bit weird. It does look great though and everyone else says it's a really nice thing to do, maybe I'm just thinking too much into it.

2:38pm I tried to find out more about how Leith's doing today in my free, but no one knew anything, so I checked the internet for news stories instead. The reports said the alcohol level in Jamie's blood was crazy high. Apparently Leith had climbed up the ravine with a broken ankle, ruptured spleen and fractured elbow to try and wave down a car. Not a broken neck then as I thought, at least that's something. They'd veered off the road and gone down an embankment at around 2:30am, but because it was dark, no passing cars could actually see them. Leith couldn't stand up to get more attention because of his ankle and spleen, so it took until the sun came up at around 7:30am for a passing fireman to see Leith waving. That must have been horrific. He was screaming for help and could see and hear the cars going past, but they couldn't see him. The article said they smashed into some trees at high speed and the car split in half killing Anna and Jamie on impact. Fuck.

6:57pm I've made mum and dad a little photo album of what camp is like day-to-day. I was addressing the envelope earlier at visual arts, when one of the other counselors was having a nose to see what I was doing.
Counselor: "Tipton-under-Trent? My friend lives there."
I thought she was winding me up, but she described the village and it turns out her best friend from university *lives* in my old house. How weird is that? I live in a tiny village and we're all the way out here in America. It's such a small world.

7:57pm Just been with Cara. She's got these flowers outside her bunk – ones that twirl in the wind – as she's in the youngest bunk and the kids forget where they live. Every night she moves them around to confuse the kids and she finds it absolutely hilarious. Her favourite part is winding up her campers in the morning about who moved them. She said today's story, to these poor innocent six year olds, is that it must have been the big bears in the woods coming down in the night to find a child to eat.

11:47pm It was the memorial for Jamie and Anna this evening. Anna's family drove down from New Jersey to come and pick up her stuff and do a speech about their 'beautiful, happy and amazing daughter'. It was horrific. Her dad said how he used to come here to see his baby girl in the shows, and now it's turned into her final resting place. He stood up there with her mum and brothers and they looked wretched.

Jamie's parents didn't come. He's definitely getting the blame for it. People say Anna would never have got in the car if she'd known he'd been drinking, but how could she not know? She must have been at the GC and saw him drinking, surely. And she can't have asked him if he'd been drinking because he wouldn't have lied to her. I just don't like how everyone is putting all the blame on him. There was no doubt the service was more for Anna, but she was better known around camp. Some counselors did readings and then they showed some photos on the projector screen that just set everyone off crying, if they weren't already. The pictures we took when we having a crafty fag up at the GC in the first week were up there, obviously the ones without cigarettes. It made me so sad to remember that fun night. We didn't know then that he only had two weeks left to live.

Anna's best friend Jess did a speech. She told us how she found out about Jamie and ran to Anna's bunk to tell her. Anna's co counselors told her that Anna hadn't come back that night either, she put two and two together and realised she must have been with him. How fucking awful. I just can't, and don't want to, imagine what I'd do if any of my best friends died. I guess you get through it somehow, but you wouldn't want to.

I don't know where Zoe was, and I don't want to get annoyed about it. I don't think she even came. Rebecca went off somewhere near the front so I was left trying to comfort our campers. It's kind of nice when they revert to seeming being all babyish and needy of my love. Makes me feel wanted.

The service was so sad, but it was good for the kids, and the counselors, to be able to say goodbye in some sort of ceremony. The accident is really hanging over camp and it sounds awful, especially considering it was only a few days ago that I was distraught, but as Earl has told us, the camp has to move on. Kids forget quickly and he doesn't want this to affect the next session. If the kids are sad all summer, they won't come back next year.

Monday 11th July

9:02am Argh fucking Zoe! She just lies in bed all the time. I actually have to make her go and teach her lessons; she's a joke!

12:17pm At breakfast I have to get the girls to choose their three minors for the day. Getting them to decide and fill in the sheet is an absolute nightmare.

Them: "Yeah, yeah Lucy, whatever. I'll do it in a minute."

When they do have the sheet they'll spend ages poring over the possibilities and then the other girls don't have time to fill it in. You can't let them go until they've done it, because the front office has to make a register with all the activity codes for the rest of the day so they know where the kids are at any given time. Well, where they should be. In the end I just put them down for anything, so the front office has their precious code. I know they won't turn up anyway – a girl I teach in leather was telling me how one of the campers' tricks is to bring loads of covers and blankets so they can sleep in their bunk on their break and hide under them. I'm going to be well on the lookout for this now. They either do that or just go and find somewhere to sit and hide at camp – probably behind the portaloos, or up in the theatre rafters, or another secret somewhere I don't know about. The head counselors are pretty strict about skiving though – they patrol the bunks during lesson time and boot out any kids that are in there and make them go to their majors and minors. The kids are pretty free to do what they want on camp – as long as they go to lessons and are in bed on time that is – it's not like the counselors have to drop them off or anything, they're trusted to get there by themselves.

I spoke to the head counselor about changing bunks.

Head counselor: "I can try, but it'll just be another set of problems you know."

I guess she's right. It's not like Cara and Emily are having the greatest time in the world with the younger kids. She said she knows I've got the most difficult girls on camp and understands how hard it is, but she'd try and help with them more. I might as well just try and make the most of it I suppose. They do seem to be being nicer to me since the accident anyway.

Another thing that's making me feel down at the moment is teaching crafts with the old South African woman, she's such a bitch. She's probably about 60, but it's like she sees me as a child and doesn't trust me to do anything. I really, really don't know why she's here. She looks so grumpy all the time and I'm sure she hates children. I hate, hate, hate teaching that lesson with her.

7:12pm I was walking away from the radio shack to go and have a sleepy in my bunk earlier and I saw Ben sat on the grass outside my bunk. He was obviously waiting for me so I jumped him. It was then I realised he was crying. His Nan has died. He said he could feel something had happened at breakfast time so he rang home and his sister said his nan had passed away in the night.

Ben: "I know she was old, but she was like a mum and a dad to me. I can't believe I won't be there for her funeral."

He's absolutely devastated. It's horrible to see him so upset; his beautiful face was scrunched up and his cheeks were stained with tears. He wasn't embarrassed to let it all out in front of me and we just sat there with me trying to comfort him with a hug. I didn't really know what to say and I could see the campers were starting to come back to the bunks ready for lunch. I hope he can use his spirituality to get through it somehow. I don't know, I hope he's ok. I don't actually know how much more sadness I can take here. We all need some more fun in our lives.

8:16pm Camper: "Lucy, how far have you gone with a boy?"
Me: "Errrrm, errrrrrm, none of your business."
Then one of the 13-year-olds told me she'd slept with her boyfriend.
Camper: "Well, we have been going out for three years."
Wow.

I was asking them about what they do for fun – they don't seem to be into alcohol at all. If I'd come to camp with all my mates at 13 I'd have definitely sneaked a bottle or two in. These kids have never mentioned anything about booze – they've talked about drugs quite a bit though. Apparently they're much easier to get hold of because of the 21 drinking age. I guess getting pissed is a bigger thing in England; they're all stoners here instead.

9:36pm It amazes me how close the girls are here. They're so open with each other, talking about their feelings and sharing their experiences of growing up. I remember when I was their age and everything was so secret in my group of friends. We wouldn't talk about the pressures or weirdness of growing up at all; we'd just fall out when we were upset or stressed and not talk to each other. It seems so bizarre now. I remember at 15, one of my friends' parents split up, she'd only ever talk about it when we were drunk. I genuinely feel our inability and reluctance to talk to each other has stunted my emotional growth.

In our free lessons together Ben tries to get me to talk about my feelings, but it feels weird. All through school and university I'd always like guys way out of my league for one reason or another – too old, too fit, attached – then I'd build them into something they weren't and think about how great we'd be together if only they'd give me a chance. If a guy ever did like me I'd find some reason why I didn't like them. To actually like a boy and have them feel the same about me feels pretty amazing, but I don't actually know how to deal with it.

9:49pm Earlier we were sat on my bed and the kids were talking about their bikini lines, and how wide they were growing and whether to shave them or not. Obviously I stayed out of that one – bit weird – but then they lifted up their little shorts to show each other! What the fuck?

These girls have even started taking showers together, and those cubicles are small. They argue about who's going to go in with who. There was definitely no need to worry that I'd make them feel self-conscious or worried about me seeing them half naked in the bunk, they let it all hang out.

11:07pm I've got this camper who really reminds me of myself at that age. I don't think any of the counselors would describe her as nice or kind, but I'm sure her friends would. She's pretty horrible to me as well, but I can see that she really cares about her friends. She's cheeky, funny and lazy – just like me at 13. She's always asking why she has to do things and being really shitty, and then trying another approach and is really sweet and nice to me to try and get out of doing stuff. She just wants to hang out with her friends and have fun up at canteen. I do like her but she gives me *a lot* of aggro. God, I'm feeling horrifically sorry for my ex-teachers right now.

Tuesday 12th July

2:15pm Everyone's started hanging out in the staff room a lot more since the accident. I think it's a mixture of not wanting to be around the kids so much and the fact that all the counselors have got a lot closer since it happened.

The staff room is pretty cool; it's divided into two. On one side are three sofas and a big TV, that's where the toilet is too, which stinks. I'd hate to know how many counselors have had sex in there. On the other side is a desk with two computers that never work, the phone booths, a pool table with half the balls missing and a foosball table. The windows are those ones where you can see out and not in – for the kids protection as much as ours I think. Everyone just sits around eating and chatting. Bud and Earl never come in here – probably because it smells like a garbage dump.

7:12pm Just found out some of the Mean Girls will be staying for six weeks. I'm *absolutely* gutted. Bah!

On a more fun note: we had a carnival for lazy day today. Each bunk set up a stall on the big green and the campers and counselors just had to go around and try them all. Basically, it's just an easy day of playing around with no majors or minors to teach. Danielle beat the shit out of me on the pillow duel game. We each had to stand on a podium and then smack each other with a pillow until one of us falls. Ben and Cara were pissing themselves laughing at Danielle and me trying to overthrow each other. Pete was chucking the extra cushions at me to try and knock me off and Pip had the kids chanting, "Lucy, Lucy, Lucy". Obviously Danielle only won because I'm so nice and didn't want to hurt her – she's about 5ft nothing compared to my 5ft 9. After this, to show there were no hard feelings, we got married by a 10-year-old dressed as a vicar in the gay wedding booth. I had to wear a veil and hold a bouquet and Danielle wore a top hat while we had our photos taken. There was a straight one too – but it wasn't anywhere near as busy.

I went to the Hershey's Chocolate Kisses stall where you could send a 'kiss' to someone in the internal mail. The campers whose idea it was gave them out at dinnertime with labels attached that people had been writing during the day, it was very sweet. One of my campers found out I'd sent one to Ben; she found it hilarious so decided to take the piss out of me for the rest of the day.

I got to know Pip a lot better today – she's a funny fucker. She manages to take the piss out of the campers without them actually realising, but she's not actually being mean. They just don't get our sense of humour or understand our jokes, which makes them even funnier to me.

8:47pm Watched Camp Rockbear American Idol tonight for evening activity, at the Kennedy Theatre. There's this girl at camp called Alexis who's about 17 and gorgeous, and all the other girls totally worship her. They follow her around and try to spot her like she's some celebrity.

Britney, longingly: "Alexis is so beautiful. I actually want to be her."

She's so pretty and has the coolest clothes – I think I might hate her. She didn't win, even though every girl on camp was rooting for her. Ron and Earl chose some guys who'd made up a dance routine to go with their song too. She was crushed; everyone thought she was a dead cert. God, even I'm starting to take these things seriously.

My campers this session aren't really into the performing arts side of this err, performing arts camp, so I don't think I'm seeing what the other counselors are. When I go to Danielle's bunk with the 16-year-olds, or even Emily's with the eight-year-olds, they're all practicing their lines and warming up their voices in the mornings. Their kids put loads of pressure on themselves to get the parts – apparently when the leads went up on the notice boards on the second day they were up at 6am checking to see if they were up yet. My kids just aren't into that. They can't even be bothered to go to breakfast, never mind an audition.

9:30pm Christ. The girls in the bunk opposite are having a bra party! They're 15 and all dressing up in their bras and knickers to hang out together. They're doing filthy poses and taking pictures of each other on the terrace. The kids are just so confident with their bodies and with each other here. I'm leaving this mad house for my night off, woohoo!

Wednesday 13th July

10am On my way to New York City! It was my night off last night so Ben and me just slept in the staff room. He's still really upset about his Nan so we didn't feel like going out. Loads of people sleep in there. I think we're allowed, but it's not really encouraged. All the Polish do it because they signed up to come and work in the kitchen and didn't realise they'd have to sleep in the bunks with the kids. Having them in the bunks is rubbish for the kids too though as kitchen staff have to get up at about 5am, and their alarms wake everyone up.

We've just heard that Leith is going to be fine. Obviously he's just going back home to Scotland rather than coming to camp, he must be traumatised. He's got pins holding his ankle together. It's only been nine days since they died, but sadly things have definitely moved on. Time is slow, but also fast at camp; a day seems like a week and a week a month. Since the memorial the kids haven't talked about Jamie and Anna at all. Everything is pretty much back to normal, although Earl still hasn't opened the GC. I'm sure Anna and Jamie's families don't feel like things have moved on at all, but we have to. This is meant to be a kid's paradise, not a place where counselors crash into trees.

8:17pm Had a brilliant time in New York. It's about a four-hour drive away – driver John dropped us off and picked us up on a mini bus, as usual. We went up the Empire State Building – it was amazing. And we went to Greenwich Village and walked around the little boutique stores. We saw Carrie's steps off *Sex and the City* and got a photo sat on them. Emily and me bought loads of sweets from the massive Toys r Us in Times Square and a few hot dogs from the street vendors. We got a quick look at Central Park – it was just like the movies where people walk their dogs, run, skate, chat. I'm gutted we didn't see any celebrities, but it really was amazing. I'm excited to explore it more after camp.

I can't help but spend loads of money when I'm on my days off and judging by the amount of bags on the bus no one else can either. It's the one time we're free to do, eat, say and spend what we want, so everyone just goes crazy.

Thursday 14th July

9:17am The head counselor just came round and told us we have to be more vigilant with the campers in the evenings. Last night Bud was patrolling in his gator and his headlights lit up one of the girls sucking off a guy in the bushes. Haha, busted! How mortifying for them. The new rules are that the boys aren't allowed to touch the brown bits of the girls bunks – the stairs, porch, window frames, stairs – and vice versa. Not really sure how that will stop them getting together, but the kids seem to find it very funny that Earl and Bud have told them they'll get pregnant if they touch them.

There are so many stories about what these kids get up to – it's pretty funny. One boy was telling me about the 'Mountain Dew challenge'. Every time you manage to get a blowjob you buy a can of Mountain Dew, drink it and line it up with the others on the rafter above your bed in the bunk. Whoever fills their rafter first, wins. I hope the girls aren't feeling pressured to do stuff with the boys. Some of these girls are so beautiful and the teenage boys are just gross, spotty and feral.

The kids also seem to think hickeys are cool. Some of them are covered in purple and brown bruises all up their necks. It's so disgusting, but they actually compete to see who can get the most.

12:23pm I still find it really difficult to get the girls up in time for breakfast and to get them out the bunk to their majors and minors. It wears me out before I've even started the day. This is a normal morning once Rebecca has woken up first and gone into the bathroom, and after I've managed to haul my normally hungover self out of bed at around 7:30am:

Me: "Right everyone, time to get up."

(no answer)

Me: "Come on!"

The girls: (murmurs and grumbles from under the covers)

Me (walking around and shaking them): "Please, come on, get up. We need to leave in five minutes/breakfast is calling/it's time to start the day."

Them (from under the duvet): "Jeez Lucy, shut up! We're getting up!"

Me: "Come on! Get up! It's time for breakfast!"

It continues like this until I'm ready to throttle someone. The head counselor comes round to make sure the counselors are up and then leaves it to us to get them out. In the end Rebecca takes the ones who are ready up to breakfast and I stick around for the rest of them. Otherwise they're like dominoes and will all just fall back in bed and under the covers. Note how Zoe has sweet FA to do with all this. If everyone could be trusted to get up and to breakfast straight away, we could technically get up five minutes before we had to be there seeing as we're not far away, but they can't.

It's so hard to get their respect and to get them to listen to you. I think it's because we're so close in age, they're just not interested and they don't think they have to respect us. As soon as one of the head counselors speaks, they listen. Obviously they've got more respect than us because they're heads, but I also think it's because they're that bit older too – that five or so years makes all the difference.

I'm definitely getting on better with them now though. I think I just need to remember what I was like at their age – lazy and selfish – and that's pretty much them. They're happy to lie in bed and watch me sweep and mop the bunk floor out of sheer frustration and they don't care that they live in a pigsty. The other day I picked all the clothes off the floor and dumped them all on the spare bed. Five minutes later they'd ripped them all down again and were moaning at me for 'touching their stuff'. I really don't know what to do about them – I wish I could just let them get on with it, but the head counselor will be well pissed off if I don't at least try to get them to lessons.

6:58pm I really like how close Cara and Ben are. Emily doesn't like him – she thinks he's a bit weird with all his talk of clairvoyance and spirituality. But him and Cara really get on and they seem to find each other hilarious.

7:09pm Zoe keeps disappearing in rest hour to go running, leaving Rebecca and me to look after the kids. She's really, really pissing me off. She doesn't think about anyone else, ever. Everything she does is just to please herself. Her and Pip came up to play in jewellery in their free today; they did actually make some really cool stuff. You could see Rebecca was raging though – blatantly jealous of how good their creations were. She just kept muttering under her breath about them using supplies that were meant for the kids and asking why they were even here. Rebecca just teaches the kids to thread beads on string and jewellery is just seen as a place to hang out, not anywhere to actually get creative. Pip and Zoe were sculpting the wire to make really detailed necklaces and just adding a bead or two here and there to make it classier. That showed Rebecca anyway, she really thinks she knows it all. Don't think it did Zoe any favours with her though.

Pip is brilliant. She comes a close second to Cara in funniness stakes. She tells me all these hilarious stories about camping in the Australian outback and getting fucked on drugs and booze around campfires. It sounds like her life is all mad parties, bonfires and barbecues. The kids in her bunk absolutely love her – I would if she was my bunk counselor. She's reassuringly mum-like in that she's a big girl, but then she's super silly and always joking around too – the perfect counselor. I'd probably find it annoying to be her co-counselor in a bunk, as she's just not bothered about what the kids do, or about getting them to lessons. I guess it's similar to working with Zoe, that's probably why they're such good friends. I love her up at visual arts though – the stuff she gets the kids doing is well impressive.

9:16pm I went to Danielle's bunk in rest hour. I was appalled by how clean, tidy and spotless it was. She's brilliant with her campers – they're a bit older than mine, not that that means anything in terms of tidiness – but by the looks of it, she's got them well whipped into shape. You can tell by looking at Danielle she's a really neat and tidy person: her make up is flawless and even though she works on the climbing wall her nails are always perfect too. She's the only person I know at camp who carries lip-gloss around with her and she's also the only person I've seen in heels while we've been here. She thought it was funny that I was so shocked by her bunk, so I invited her to come to mine and survey the shit tip we like to call F13B.

Danielle: "Eugh, how can you live like this?" as she picked up a skanky crumpled top between her finger and thumb.

She was disgusted, but my campers found it really funny. I did too, a little bit. But as I looked around to survey what the bunk looked like to her, I noticed the wet and dirty towels stinking of river water draped over the rafters, knickers falling out the half-closed drawers, clothes hanging onto the shelves by threads, photos scattered across the floor, bare blu tac on the walls and enough cosmetics to stock a small chemist strewn across the empty bunks.

Danielle: "Is that towel dry? Fold it. And that one."

Camper: "It's not m---"

Danielle: "Fold it. After you've done that make that bed."

And before I knew it, she'd got my bunk sparkling. It was like Mary Poppins was in the room with her little birdies. Damn, I'm a shit counselor.

Little bitch camper Britney was having a fit earlier. Someone has drunk one of her Fiji waters that she'd bought to camp especially. I think she's only had two in three weeks, but no one else is allowed them. She's going mental accusing all the other kids. I just left her to it; it was pretty funny to watch from the safety of my top bunk. Fuck, I hope my child is nothing like her.

11:53pm Eugh, Britney just made me tuck her in and give her a cuddle. It'd be sweet from anyone else, but I'm sure she's doing it to mock me. She knows the hierarchy at camp: Earl at the peak, the paying campers next, then Bud and a few others such as Earl's wife, then it's the senior staff, then the horses, and then the counselors.

What the campers say and do goes, if you have a complaint made about you, you're out. We're dispensable and she knows this. Bitch.

Friday 15th July

9:13am Getting the girls to breakfast is one of the hardest parts of being a camp counselor without a doubt. I don't want to be up – especially after a boozy night – and I have to get a load of angsty 13-year-olds up and showered too. It's so cold in the mornings, you'd do anything to be able to stay in bed, except feel the wrath of Earl that is. It's a freezing cold walk up to the dining hall so everyone dresses in hoodies, then by the time breakfast is finished the sun's out and you've got that familiar, sick, claustrophobic feeling of being too hot and eating too many delicious mini bagels laced with full-fat cheese.

After we've had breakfast and gone back to the bunk it's usually even worse. The kids are all in carb comas so just want to get back in bed, but you have to get them up and cleaning the bunk. It needs to be swept and scrubbed and all their clothes folded up neatly. There's nothing I want more than to go back to bed for an hour before classes start, but I have to shout at them to get up and get cleaning. If we did it straight away when we got back we could probably get a half-hour kip in, but they answer back, or even worse just ignore me and look at me like I'm shit. I have to keep nagging them and I get sick of the sound of my own voice.

Rebecca is so miserable these days. The kids' cleanup is never good enough for her, and she barely speaks to anyone anymore. It's like she's turned into a grumpy teenager. She's so stroppy and mardy; I don't know what her problem is. Actually, I think her main problem with me today is the fact that I've broken her necklace she leant me. Better not tell her it happened when I was getting frisky with Ben then, oops.

12:45pm Every few days the girls have shaving parties. They'll get little pots of water each, go on the porch, sit in a line and slap the foam on to shave their legs communally. During today's shaving party one of my campers told me her parents said for every pound she loses at camp they'd give her $100! She's probably a size 10ish and very healthy and athletic-looking. What the hell?

My stained glass class is going ok. I don't know what the

parents will say when they see pieces of glass stuck to a square of wood, but at least the kids are having fun.

6:56pm Leather is definitely my favourite lesson to teach. It doesn't require any of these skills everyone has apart from me, and I'm actually quite creative in it. I teach with Cara at the end of the day and Ben sits next-door teaching drawing, so I like going in to see him every now and then. His kids are always so quiet in there – he says all he can hear is me and Cara screeching about being careful with hammers and the kids squealing when they hit themselves with them. There are only a few kids in his class, but he has such a good rapport with each of them. They love him. He's like a gentle giant and he's so calming to be around – perfect for an arts teacher. He's a lot of fun without being too brash or in your face. I swear one of the girls is into him though. She's very pretty, for a 15-year-old, and always gives me filthy looks when I go in to see him. I'd say she's definitely got a soft spot for him. I love having Ben and Cara as my best friends here. It's nice to know you've always got someone supporting you and who likes you best out of everyone.

Anyway, back to leather – generally we get the kids to make belts or bracelets.

- I'll cut them a piece of leather and show them how to dye it.
- They dye it and wait for it to dry, messing around in the meantime.
- Next, they use stamps and a hammer to stamp pictures and letters into the leather. Or they can use a scalpel to cut sections out.

That's it.

Leather is simple and cool, and the kids love it because they have something they'll actually use to take home with them. I've even made a few little gifts for myself in the form of about ten belts and a few bracelets for some select friends. The leather department is right next to the computer room too, so Cara and me are in a nice little rhythm of covering for each other while we each go and check our emails every day. I feel so sorry for the guy in there. He has around 20 computers to maintain, the only reason the kids go in there is to play on MySpace and email their friends, and the internet connection is unbelievably shit. It never works so he has 20 kids in there with fierce computer rage. He doesn't look like he copes with it all very well either.

7:25pm Cara's just been to the bunk slagging off some of the counselors who arrived in the second session. She's definitely a love her or hate her person. I love her, I wish I could work with her all the time, but I think she's a bit much for the other counselors to cope with. She says random stuff around the kids and other counselors turn their noses up.
Cara: "Earl's a dirty great roide, isn't he Lucy?"
Haha, oh she does make me laugh.

When she's annoyed about something her face is so earnest and sincere, but then what comes out her mouth is something totally different. She swears like a fisherman's wife – never around the kids though, well hardly ever. She's obviously not impressed at being left in visual arts, but has just decided to have fun no matter what. The visual arts boss will tell her to do something, she'll start it, and then wander off when she sees something more fun going on.

Some days she comes in and I can tell she's in a good, pro-active mood. She'll tidy the cupboards and get the kids in order and listening, and she won't take any shit. Then other days she'll come in and just let the kids do whatever they want and walk around cleaning up after them. I guess it's when she's tired. Actually, everyone looks completely exhausted – how the hell are we going to last all summer – there's still six weeks to go?

7:43pm The kids are going *Harry Potter* crazy; it's all they can talk about. The new book comes out tomorrow so the doting parents are sending it straight to camp via special delivery. As of tomorrow Earl's even introduced a *Harry Potter* minor into the schedule so the kids can sit and read their books during the day. Not my girls though, oh no, they're too cool to read.

Mealtime post is *so* competitive. It's like a popularity contest between whose parents love them the most. I note that my parents haven't actually sent me anything yet. One of the English counselors got some Cadbury's chocolate in the post the other day; she was really sweet and gave it out to everyone. The chocolate in America is shit – Hershey's is horrible. If I come next year I'm definitely going to bring some choccy to win some friends, although it probably wouldn't even last the flight with me, nom nom.

8:19pm Zoe told me earlier that she's actually friends with the head of the drama department here back home in Australia. He told her she should come to this camp and she'd meet some rich and famous kids with celebrity parents who could offer her a big acting break. I don't think he counted on her actually coming out though. Now he's not talking to her and she's really upset. I think she's treading on his ground, or some shit like that. I feel sorry for her, but it was a pretty stupid thing to do. I didn't think anyone actually came here for a career move, well I guess teachers do, but not wannabes. Sounds like she had a lot counting on it.

I wonder if that's why she's always singing and doing OTT monologues in the bunk? She must be desperately trying to get the kids' attention so they can tell their imaginary influential parents about her. Hmmm, don't think that's going to work somehow.

We've got three days left of this session. I'll be glad to say bye to some of these girls, but because so many are staying it doesn't really feel like the end of anything this time round.

Saturday 16th July

7:31am Bud's still going every day with that fucking loudspeaker... Loudspeaker: "Eeeeeeeeeeeevvverybody up, up, up! It's time to riiiise and shiiine... It's a beautiful day on the Rockbear campus..."

4:30pm The kids are cottoning onto the fact the water trampoline is *brilliant*. There never used to be any campers down there, but now it's always busy and the lifeguard boss doesn't let counselors use it if there are too many paying campers there. I have to sit on the picnic bench and write in my diary instead.

There's this counselor – I don't actually even know his real name – everyone just calls him Cowboy because of his Stetson. He's super fit and walks around either topless with jeans and cowboy boots or with his camp-issue t-shirt on. No one wears that camp-issue t-shirt like he does. He swaggers around camp and it's like an imaginary dreamy, smoky haze follows him. I'm too star-struck to speak to him. Things are still going well with Ben. It's like we're 'going steady' although nothing official. I like him. A lot.

Sunday 17th July

11am Eugh, looking at Danielle's co counselor today at breakfast I literally hated myself. She's so perfect. It must be lovely to swan through life being so tall, slim and naturally beautiful. I bet she doesn't go to the GC with the intention of drinking as much as possible, or scoff pizza at night canteen, or have dirty booze poos in portaloos. Damn, must be more like her.

7:13pm It's changeover today and all the parents have been to see their little cherubs in their shows to see what their $4,000 has got them. Seeing as most of my kids are staying to next session, their parents were just here to visit for the day.

We had an art show with the best items from all the art departments in the lower arts block. The kids are so proud to see their work on the walls and it looks great framed – even the crappy attempts from mine and Cara's stained glass class look good against a white background. The visual arts boss got some drinks and snacks and we set them out on the tables. As counselors we're responsible for welcoming the mums and dads and showing them around. Cara was up to her old tricks with knowing everyone in Ireland, it turns out the parents are as stupid as the children.
Sample parent: "We're a 14th Irish, we're related to Maggie O'Donnell, do you know her?"
Cara: "Ah yes, what was her son called again? Ah yes, wonderful woman."
Haha. She's got balls has Cara.

I swear on parents' day all these campers come along to introduce me to their family and I've never, ever seen them before. I've become an expert at blagging it. I just tell the parents how great their child is and how much they've developed at camp, and they buy it. They love feeling their thousands of dollars is making their child a better person.

No sign of Keakuki's parents today, poor girl.

It's sad that unless you say bye to the kids at least two days before the end of the session you'll miss out. The changeover day of camp is so hectic: I have to run a few classes at visual arts for the kids staying over into next session, but also be at the bunk to say goodbye to the ones who are leaving and hello to the new arrivals. This means the kids who want to say bye don't know where to find you. I need to be better prepared next changeover day.

11pm The food changes so much when the parents are in town. The fried chicken we've been eating all month has miraculously been replaced with vibrant salads, and you can actually choose vegetables rather than between fries or mash.

I didn't get to see Ben all day we were both so busy. Usually I'm guaranteed a sighting at meal times, but on changeover days they extend the meal times so you can go up any time in a two-hour period, so I missed him there too.

I watched a few of the shows and I'm still just absolutely amazed at the kids' talent. When I was a child I wanted to be on the stage, at one point it was actually my life's goal to be in a West End show. I think I knew then and I definitely know now, I would absolutely, definitely never have made it. These kids are *incredible*.

Session Three

Monday 18th July

12.15pm Ahhhhh! David Corraddi's* [super famous actor I can't reveal] kids are in the bunk just opposite mine. The head counselor has already said we're not allowed to ask them about him though. Cannot *wait* for parents' day.

Changeover day today – got $260 in tips, not bad! Should get me an iPod from the dodgy janitor anyway. All the kids have got them and they look amazing, you can store so much music and they're much smaller than my discman.

Half the Mean Girls have gone and half are staying, I hope they'll be a bit easier to talk to and cope with now there aren't so many of them. The parents of the ones who are staying for six weeks came to see how they were getting on and it was surprisingly cute to see them together. You wouldn't suspect all the grief they've caused me these past few weeks. I wish my parents could come and visit for the weekend, I miss them.

The new girls seem lovely. One of the new campers' parents obviously didn't want to leave her with us heathens; they were so hesitant to go. We must look like crazed wild animals with cabin fever by now. My hair is thick and bushy and my roots are a disgrace, my clothes are filthy and I've never seen the circles under my eyes so dark.

Rebecca, Zoe and me got the new girls settled in and tried to assimilate them into the bunk with little bitch Britney and co who have stayed behind. I hope they're going to all get on this session – it could go either way. We've got two emo kids who came together, two from Miami, one blonde speccy kid, a posh one – she's the one whose parents didn't want to leave her – and a super nerd. Along with Britney and her entourage, this could be a recipe for disaster, or maybe opposites will attract, we'll see.

9:16pm For the sake of the children I thought I better sort the barnet out – I was scaring myself to look in the mirror. I'm sure the new kids think I'm a bit weird walking around with dye on my hair though – I bet their mummies don't use DIY boxes. There is a camp hairdresser who comes at the end of each session, but money's a bit tight what with spending it all up at the GC and in Walmart. I'll sort the roots, but the bushy, wild effect will have to wait until home.

I watched the staff football game in rest hour with Emily. We just chatted about boys – much more fun than actually playing them. Apparently last night two people were caught shagging in the pit where they tie-dye all the clothes up at visual arts. Rumour's going around that it was me and Ben – need to put a stop to that one! Haha, pretty funny though, everyone here is pure filth.

Just getting ready for my night and day off...

Tuesday 19th July

9:19pm All of us alternate dayers went to Kingfisher Falls again for the night yesterday. Driver John took us via Walmart and the wine shop to get some supplies, and then dropped us down there with our sleeping bags and swimming stuff. It definitely felt like a disaster waiting to happen with all of us cooking sausages on the open fire, in high spirits and getting pissed next to the river. We had the bonfire going to keep us warm and we just sat around chatting. There are these bunks down there with one side missing so anyone can sleep in them. They don't have beds or anything and there's not enough room to stand up, but they're perfect for one night in the wilderness. Pete and me decided to go skinny-dipping, until he tried to get me to touch his pierced willy, gross!

Anna's best mate Jess is in a right state. I shared a bunk with her and she was talking manically and crushing up her anti-depression drugs to make lines to snort. As soon as I met her in about week two I was fascinated by her – she seemed so interesting and complicated. Even seeing her in that state I still thought she was cool. She's so confident and fun and everyone at camp loves her – for some reason I feel like her issues and angst make her even cooler. My life is just boringly simple in comparison, although I know if something like this happened to me I'd fall apart. I look at people like her – before Anna died – and I think they must be having the best life. She's loved and slim and beautiful – all the things I want in life. I guess just because she has all the things I want doesn't mean she's happy, she wants something else. I need to remember this.

One minute she was talking quickly and crazily and the next she was laying on the floor spaced out. She said everything in her life was a mess before, and now that her best friend has died it could be the final thing to push her over the edge, of sanity and towards suicide, I assume. She hasn't accepted the death; she's a wreck. Everybody else has allowed themselves to move on. It was a horrific accident that happened so quickly a lot of counselors hadn't even had time to get to know Jamie, Anna and Leith. For Jess though, Anna was ingrained in her life. They're best friends from home and have been coming to camp together for years – she won't be able to get over it so quickly.

Seeing her in that state brought everyone down. We ended up getting so drunk and morose that we just fell asleep. We woke up in the morning a bit hazy, but ready to go to Truhampton where I spent the day eating and shopping my way around the mall. I printed some photos off my new camera at the chemist of camp so far and I've got some really nice ones of Ben and me – we look good together. He's so tall and muscular; sexy. I just kept looking through them on the way back to camp; Danielle was taking the piss out of me big style. She's blatantly just jealous.

1:45am Aww, just got back from being with Ben. He'd organised it with the waterfront staff that one of the canoes would be on the other side of the lake from the camp. He asked me to come with him on a midnight walk and then took me out in it in the moonlight. He had a whisky miniature for us to share – it was the most romantic thing anyone's ever done for me. It was so perfect. We could hear the squeals and noises from camp from afar, but really it was silent apart from the odd cricket in the grass or lap of water as the fish swam around us. He'd bought some hoodies with him so I didn't even notice the cold once we were in the canoe. He paddled us out a bit and we had a smooch. Ahh, it was amazing!

Wednesday 20th July

9:09am I swear, as soon as my head hits the pillow at night I just conk out. I've never slept so well as I do here, I'm exhausted by the time I get in bed. I remember those first nights at camp when I couldn't sleep – it genuinely feels like a lifetime ago. The kids could run a riot now for all I know about them after hours.

My new schedule has started. The visual arts boss was quite nice about the scheduling, although a bit weird at the same time...

Her: "I've given you and Cara the same period off as I know you're best friends and like to hang out together all the time."

Hmmm, felt like she was getting at us a bit there. She was doing that classic bitchy girl thing of disguising a mean dig with a kind overtone. Whatever, at least we get to teach a few lessons together. This is my day in session three...

Major 1: Rocketry with Cara
Minor 1: Photo with Rebecca
Minor 2: Radio BY MYSELF
Major 2: Crafts with Cara
Minor 3: Off
Major 3: Jewellery with a few of the second session counselors.

Zoe's still not bothering to do any work in the bunk and trying to get her up in the morning is a nightmare. I'm actually doing her a favour by waking her up and getting her out of the bunk every morning, but I know she thinks I'm getting at her. Why doesn't she just get the fuck out of bed when the rest of us do? Apparently they're getting well pissed off with her up at drama as well. She needs to be careful; Earl won't stand for any of this shit if he hears about it.

The leftover Mean Girls and the new kids are actually getting on really well, I'm shocked! Britney is being really nice and even sharing her Fiji waters with them. Mornings have got easier and everyone seems to be a lot happier. The two little ones from Miami – Alexa and Stephanie – are so sweet. They're always dancing around the bunk and they're so lovely, and funny too. I think they've taken a shine to me; at breakfast they chose their minors especially so they could spend them with me. Stephanie's got this white-blonde wild hair that always makes her look a bit scrappy. She is girly, but in a tomboy sort of way. She's just not into clothes, or boys or fashion and she always seems like she's in a bit of a fairy world. She's got coloured braces on her teeth, but she'll be stunning when she's older, you can tell. Alexa is the more grown up out of the two. They're cousins, but best friends too – I'm sure she'll lead Stephanie astray at some point in their lives. Alexa has an eye for the boys and enjoys dressing up in slutty clothes in the bunk – making her skirt shorter by rolling it up and tucking the bottom of her t-shirt over and in to make a bra top. Those old chestnuts. She's still very sweet behind all that though, they both are. They're just two normal teenagers growing up and enjoying being at camp.

1:55pm Emily and me are going to start running in the mornings. We're going to meet at 7am to run around the camp lake – I'm guessing it's about three miles – we'll see how it goes. I need to do something, I'm eating and drinking so much here, I can't believe I thought it would be a detox. All this fatty food is pumping up my thighs a treat. I cannot go back to England fatter than when I left.

In 'sunshine time' today the other counselors were talking about their art qualifications. Cara and me are the only counselors in visual arts without any. I never registered that everyone else was actually *trained* in all this creative joy, I just thought they were blagging it like us. This explains a lot.

After lunch Ben came to see me in the bunk and we were joking around about how boys aren't allowed in the bunk even if they're counselors. And then he came up the steps, through the side door and out the front. It genuinely felt so naughty. The girls were squealing and my heart was racing. It's funny how ingrained the rules can be. We're institutionalised – all it was, was Ben walking through, but I felt like he was committing a crime and I actually got a rush from it. Mmmm, bad boy hey?

7:13pm Me, Pip and Zoe have just worked out how much we get paid an hour. I'm working 12 weeks rather than nine so it's a bit different for me compared with them, but for the whole summer I get $1200, which is about £700. If I divide this by 12 it's £58 a week, my week is over six days long, but I'll say six to make things easy, so that's £9.72 per day. Each day is about 15 hours long, which is a grand total of about 65p an hour. Wow! We get food and board and no one was doing it for the money in the first place, but to work that out makes me pretty sad. I hope this is the hardest I will ever work in my life, it better be.

8:38pm Just been talking to one of the Mean Girls – who's not so mean anymore – she's desperate to go home. She was telling me that all she wants is to spend time with her dad. Her mum died when she was young and she thinks he pays for her to come to camp so he doesn't actually have to be with her. She wanted to come for three weeks to see Britney and everyone, but she says he saw it as an opportunity to get rid of her for longer. She's the one with the diamond watch – sounds like a case of poor little rich girl to me. Whatever happens, I've learnt that kids are never happy with their parenting.

11:45pm I really don't like the way Rebecca treats her supposed best friend Jo. Jo is absolutely lovely and is such a great friend to Rebecca with all her whining and misery, but Rebecca just uses her when there's no one 'cooler' around. As soon as someone more interesting comes along she drops her straight away. A few of us were sat at the canteen earlier and Rebecca was boasting about how she and Jo were going to spend some 'quality time' together tonight because they're 'best friends', blah blah. No one cares, but she likes to share these things. Then one of the kitchen staff came along and asked if anyone wanted to go to her bunk for a few beers – so we all did. It was obvious Jo didn't want to go, she's a good girl and of course you're not allowed to drink on camp, but she came anyway as I presume she wanted to spend this 'quality time' with Rebecca. Then one of the guys asked if anyone wanted to go to town, as there was a space in the car. Rebecca was pretty much out the door and in the car with her seatbelt clicked in before he'd even got his keys out. You could see Jo was like, "What the fuck?" Rebecca thinks she's better than Jo, and the rest of us actually. I definitely don't like her attitude at the moment.

When we were at the canteen earlier Pete was taking the piss out of Danielle for not going to university – he can be a real dick sometimes. I'm not sure he's actually a very nice person really. I think I forgive him too much because he's funny. He goes to Manchester University doing some business degree or something. I hate it when people our age think you have to go university to be worth something.

1:03am Just had the midnight meeting. When I arrived Ben was waiting for me with his big, woolly hoody for me to wear. He's too cute. I sat snuggled next to him in the meeting, he smells so good and he's so warm.

Earl and Bud have found out that everyone's nicking ice cream at night.

Earl: "Don't we feed you enough?"

They give us three meals a day, pizza and ice cream in the evening and then keep the canteen open for us at night too and we still want more. We're animals, there's nothing more to say.

He also said:
– We're all getting new porch lights fitted, as apparently the campers keep getting fingered on the bunk terraces. Thankfully I've seen none of this.
– They're providing buses at night and on days off for counselors so now no one should be driving anywhere. They're not doing it on lazy days though, so I don't know what we're going to do? I guess we should just be grateful we get one for nights into town.
– We're allowed to the GC now, as long as we drink pop.
Hmmm, don't think that will catch on somehow.

Cara and me were going to go to Mexico after camp, but we just can't afford it, which sucks. It's so expensive for such a short amount of time. We're thinking Florida now, but don't know yet. Ordered my iPod today – VERY excited! I'm going to sell all my CDs to try and afford a snowboarding holiday when I get home. I really want to travel everywhere now and forever – none of this office job malarkey for me. Emily, Pip and Zoe said I should go to Oz next year and Cara might do the year-long working visa so I could stay with her while I'm over there. I want to go to Dublin to see her too, and I want to go to South Africa...

Thursday 21st July

9:13am Errmm, alarm went off at 6:45am. There was no chance I was going out in the cold to run around the lake. I saw Emily at breakfast – she didn't either. We'll do it next time though, for sure.

I put some music on in clean-up time to try and encourage the campers to get off their arses and sweep the floor. Snow Patrol came on and the two emo kids were well impressed – think I got myself some points there. The kids are generally doing what I say – it's really nice. Clean up was pretty simple today and I got them all out the bunk pretty early on. The new girls are a good influence on Britney and co. I think they're seeing me in a different and more fun light too, now that I don't just have to moan at them all the time.

One of the emo kids keeps complaining she's got 'mono' and needs to stay in bed. I think it's like tonsillitis, but when one of them gets it it spreads quickly to everyone else, so they say. I think the kids' new obsession with the word 'beej' might have something to do with this. Filthy teenagers.

12:02pm Got a gator ride earlier; it was brilliant. There's this guy on camp who's actually 30-something, but you wouldn't know it – everyone calls him Peter Pan. He'd hotwired the gator and didn't have a key so he couldn't actually stop to pick me up. I just had to jump in and out while the car was moving. He was moving pizza supplies and had to keep going back and forth from the storage to the kitchen and get the kitchen staff to throw it in the back. It was the highlight of my day. The lowlight was cleaning the bunk and finding a bloody sanitary towel down the side of one of the girls' beds. These kids are feral!

12:45pm Went to use the computers in the IT room earlier and Emily was in there. She was looking through her emails and started taking the piss out of me for the one I sent before camp.
Emily: "Ha, I thought you were a right twat with those emails."

She was pissing herself laughing. I was really polite and nice in the original emails and now that she knows me, I guess she knows I was being ever so slightly fake.
Emily: "And then when you were talking about *Neighbours* and *Home and Away* when we landed, Lucy, jeez, I tried to shake you off, but you wouldn't leave me alone."
Charming.

2:05pm Earl and Bud work so hard. They must get up at about 6am and not sleep until midnight – they've got to have a siesta, surely? They're both always at breakfast, lunch and dinner and then they spend all day driving around on their gators making sure everything is ok on camp. Any problem and they'll know about it on their walkie talkies within seconds and be straight there. I'd be exhausted if I was them and I'm guessing they're at least 30 years older than me.

6:45pm On our break Cara and me played on the water bikes down at waterfront, except she couldn't keep hers upright. She kept falling off and then I'd try and help by leaning across and holding her bike still, but then I'd fall off mine. This literally kept us entertained for the hour. Also very entertaining was Cara shitting herself every time she fell in, squealing in fear and bouncing up and down whenever something slimy brushed past her leg. She's such a tomboy one minute – wanting to ride bikes and get pissed – and then she's all pink and girly the next, perving on the counselors' ripped chests down at waterfront and shrieking at over-familiar fishies.

7:16pm Just found out that Zoe is a bulimic exerciser. She'll eat shitloads and then instead of being sick, she'll manically try to burn it off through exercise. This explains why she's always going off running or just lying in bed depressed. Rebecca said people with psychological illnesses like that stay at the mental age they were when the disorder manifested – apparently that's what happened to her sister – and that is so true about Zoe. She's just like one of the campers. It's really sad, but knowing this makes me understand her better too. I guess I need to be more sympathetic, but it's hard when she's just *so* fucking annoying.

Talking about this with Rebecca has also reinforced my suspicion that all her moaning and moping is because she's depressed about her sister being depressed. I don't know how she thinks that's going to help the situation.

It absolutely pissed it down during lunch. The girls ran back to the bunk, put on their swimming costumes, grabbed their shampoo and conditioner and went outside to wash their hair in the rain. Oh, it did make me laugh. I waved at Bud from my spot on the terrace, but he didn't look too impressed with their energy-saving creativity. The look on his face made me think it was probably best to make them come inside before he told me off.

11:45pm Ben always carries around a notebook so I asked if I could have a look earlier. I found these drawings that looked just like me.

Me (teasing but pleased): "Awww, is that supposed to me?"
Him (nonchalant): "No, that's Alana."
Me: "Alana?"
Him: "My girlfriend back home."

I was shocked into silence. First I'd heard of any fucking girlfriend! I think I actually said that out loud.

Him: "Well, we've never talked about whether we were seeing other people or not."

He said he knew I'd pulled Tim from rock shop in the first week, and so presumed we weren't anything serious. What we've had together this last month is *completely* different to snogging some guy in the first week.

Him: "We live on different sides of the world, it was never going to be anything serious."

I actually can't believe he would say that. I'd let my guard down and just thought he was a nice guy and we were both in the same situation – young, free and single – and having fun. I can't believe he's got a girlfriend. That poor girl, poor me! I know we're not forever or even beyond camp, but I'd always felt like I could trust him loads. I've never felt so close to any guy as I have him this past month. We've talked about so much I would have thought he'd mention a little thing like a girlfriend. I asked him how serious he was with her.

Him: "When I get home we're going to get really serious and give it a proper shot."

Me (in my head): "What THE fuck?"

I don't think he felt any sadness, regret or even compassion at giving me this news. I felt like he was actually trying to hurt me, which doesn't match my perception of him at all. I thought with all this 'sixth sense' bollocks, that he would be able to pick up on the fact I was really into him, and that he meant a lot more to me than just some guy from rock shop I'd snogged in the first week.

It's true we've never said we're 'official' or any of that bullshit and we're just having fun, but I thought it would all mean something. I was really enjoying what we had, but the fact he's had a girlfriend all this time has changed it all. I trusted him so much. I thought he was this amazing, honest and fun guy, but he's just looking for some 'fun' before he gets married and has babies with someone he's cheating on with me. He should have told me, what an absolute dick. I'm pissed off. I'm so angry with him for telling me like that as well.

I just had to go to the portaloo and cry. How could he not tell me in all our 'chats' that he had a girlfriend? I feel like such an idiot.

We need some distance between us. I'm too attached and I don't like him having any sort of power over me. I *know* we're not a lasting thing – I wasn't thinking I'd met the love of my life or anything, but I trusted him with all these intense emotions and he's just thrown them back at me. He knew more about me than I'll ever tell anyone again.

Friday 22nd July

11:13pm Went to NYC today to drop one of my campers off – the diamond watch girl who misses her dad – at La Guardia Airport. I felt really proud she'd chosen me to take her out of me, Rebecca and Zoe – we've got on so well all this time. I was excited to take her at first, but it was a bit more effort than I realised. We left at 5:30am and when we got there her dad hadn't booked it properly, which was stressful. She managed to board the plane in the end though.

Driver John is so much fun. We just chatted shit all day about who's with who at camp and gossiped about the summer. It was a seven-hour round trip so there was plenty of time to chat. He told me that one of the head counselors is getting it on with the receptionist – controversial. And he said it's rumoured that the dodgy janitor is Earl's illegitimate love child, haha. I don't know whether I believe that one.

We had to pick up another camper on the way back, which was rubbish. As soon as she got in the car we had to zip it. Her neighbourhood in New Jersey was *incredible*. The houses were massive with swimming pools, tennis courts and everything, shame we couldn't get out for a snoop.

When I got back another one of my campers had left – $30 deposited in the travelling bank, ker-ching! Gutted I haven't been seeing any of these $1000 tips Rebecca told me about at the start, but I mustn't be greedy.

I haven't spoken to or even seen Ben all day. I'm finding it hard to not think about him though – John's gossip earlier was a great distraction. When I think about it, it always felt like Ben just wanted to protect me and have deep and meaningful chats, which is cool, but I wanted other stuff too. I thought he was being a gentleman, but now I realise he was probably feeling guilty. I don't want to feel trashy or anything but... Argh I don't know what I want. If I ever speak to him again I think I'm just going to ask him, how or what he feels. I guess I want him to be a 'boyfriend' while I'm here, that's how I always thought of him before. But then I like to feel free too, although there's no one else I'm interested in, and now there's the whole girlfriend thing to factor in too. Argh, I don't know, I'm going round in circles. I need to talk to Emily.

In other, funnier news: one of the six-year-old kids complained about Cara today. She'd been simulating sex with an inflatable dinosaur and scared the children in the bunk. Pahhaha.

As I lie in bed writing this, little Britney and her bunk buddy are in the top bed next to mine crowded round a mini DVD player. They actually look quite sweet all snuggled up in Britney's blanket. I've changed.

Saturday 23rd July

8:13am Alarm woke me up again at 6:45am for the run. No chance. I saw Emily at breakfast and she made it up. She worked out I wasn't coming and so went by herself. I feel bad.

11:58am In photography three kids were shooting what were pretty much semi porn shots. They had handcuffs on, shirts off and top hats perched. We were helping to direct them. Really not sure about what Bud and Earl would say about this one if they'd walked in, although the kids knew more than us anyway.

Cara's managed to skank loads of stuff off her kids from last session – they might only be six, but some of them were pretty much the same size as her.

Cara: "I've never been this well dressed in moy loife."

She told me earlier about the day her parents found out her twin brother was gay. They were 15 and her mum and dad were out, so obviously they had a house party. Someone put the *Miss United States of America* song from *Miss Congeniality* on. Her brother strutted down the stairs of their semi-detached house in the 'nice' Catholic area of Dublin wearing Cara's clothes and make-up, singing and hamming it up wearing a feather boa round his neck. He'd just got to the bottom step facing the front door when the key in the lock went and his mum and dad walked in. The song finished and everyone just looked at each other. His friends sneaked out in the silence and that was that, outed. This story will make me laugh forever.

Cara was so horrible to her parents when she was growing up. She told me about this one time when her parents were away and she was just sat in the lounge bored. She looked around and decided she hated all the ornaments her mum had, so she got a bin bag and walked along with her hands in a scoop and shoveled them all in. Then she put the bag in the dump. My mum would go fucking *mental* if I did that.

After nights out with her mates she always invited them and half the club back to hers for after-parties. Her mum and dad would be upstairs trying to sleep while she and her new friends ate and drank the house dry downstairs. One night they set the burglar alarm off just for a laugh to wake up the street. Another time they decided to take her mum's car for a joyride round town – think that happened quite often actually. When her and her brother were at school, they were in the same class, but they had to be split up because they were such a nightmare for the teachers. I feel sorry for her parents; sound like her and her brother are nuts.

2:08pm Zoe, Rebecca, our campers and me were sat happily minding our own business at lunch today scoffing down some perogis, when this boy came over and was 'sick' all over the table. It took me a few seconds to realise it was just soup, but it was absolutely disgusting. The girls were not happy, they all sat back with open mouths and faces scrunched in repulsion. Then I saw the camera, they were making some Jackass-style film in their video class. Earl wasn't impressed either; pretty sure the video department will be getting a talking to later.

6:52pm If I sit on the far side of our bunk's table in the dining hall I can see Ben, so today I sat on the near side. I just can't be bothered with him at the moment. He's taking away from all my fun at camp and I don't even want to see his face right now.

7:06pm The girls from the first session sent us a package with loads of crisps, sweets and cookies today. How cute is that? It's so sweet that five weeks later they're still thinking about us slaving away at Camp Rockbear.

Lovely jewellery Jo keeps talking about how much she likes the guy from lighting. I wish she didn't. He's literally tried it on with *every* other girl at camp, including some of the campers. He's a charmer, but Jo's too good for him.

7:46pm I've just got off the phone to mum and I'm so sad. It's been seven weeks since I've seen her – the longest I've ever gone. I really miss her and dad. She said she might have to have an operation on her kidney, but she doesn't want to scare me. Of course I'm going to be scared. I want to go home and be with her. If anything happened to my mum or dad while I was here I don't know what I'd do. I'm starting to wonder what I'm doing working with a load of shitty kids a million miles away and spending all my time with some dickhead boy when I should be at home with them. I'm really missing them today.

8:28pm Awww, I love my campers Stephanie and Alexa. They saw I was a bit upset and so tried to cheer me up by singing stupid little songs and doing a dance. This one just shows how different the girls are to the little Jewish innocents of the first session...
Stephanie and Alexa (singing):"Stop! Don't touch me there, this is my personal square, R.A.P.E. Get the fuck away from me!"

Since I told them Cara and me want to go to Mexico after camp, they just keep saying how we're going to get raped. If we sing that song it will protect us against all raping evil, so they say. They keep trying to persuade us to come to Miami and stay with them instead. I really couldn't imagine staying with campers, but loads of counselors do. I just think it's a bit weird and I'd definitely feel awkward.

There have been a few reports of the kids having things stolen – iPods, phones, clothes. The head counselor has told us we need to make sure we keep better tabs on the kids and if we find them in the bunk when they shouldn't be there, make sure we give them a good grilling as to what they're doing. These kids are some of the richest in America; but it's just never enough is it?

9:28pm Ben tried to walk to my radio lesson with me earlier. I was giving one-word answers and just generally being off with him. I'm still pissed off; he's made me feel like a right idiot. We got to the radio shack and I didn't talk to him, so he left. I feel mean now. I guess he's right in that we'd never said we were together or anything. It's just me living in this fantasy world where for once I'm not really even thinking or worrying about the future, then he throws it back in my face. I spoke to Emily about it afterwards, we decided that next time I see him I'm going to say this:
Me: "I'm just trying to distance myself from you a bit. The other day you made me realise I think more of you than you do of me. You made me feel used and I don't like it."

This will work well with him. He always says I block my feelings so I'm sure he'll love to hear some for once. Dickhead. I've felt so shit today. Whenever I've felt shit before I've always had him to talk to, now I'm on my own and I just want to be back at home.

Sunday 24th July

12:36pm I love it when no kids turn up for your class. You get to sack it off and have a sleep, or update your diary from the comfort of your bed.

Went to the GC last night, the first time since the accident. It was all right actually. Me, Cara, Danielle, Emily and a few other girls wore t-shirts saying, 'We think your tractor's sexy' in response to the boys' 'Do you like my tractor?' ones they were wearing around camp the other day. Cara, Danielle and a few of the other girls got them on their day off for us. I felt honoured they'd got one for me, they didn't get one for Rebecca – you could tell she was well pissed off. She likes to think everyone worships her, because I think everyone kind of did at the start of camp, before they got to know her. She was like a camp oracle. She made some snide remark about how stupid they were and strutted off. Meooww.

It was a 'nice' night, pretty non-eventful compared to the old nights up there. I guess everyone's being more cautious, and it feels weird to be getting back to normal when two people have died. Danielle pulled one of the fitties from waterfront; she's getting around a bit that girl!

I saw a skunk, which was exciting – they look just like the cartoons.

Ben and me didn't speak. When I got there he was sat at a table on the terrace. He saw me, I smiled then went in to get a round, and when I came out he'd gone home. Bit weird and unnecessary.

Had a really fun morning today. Cara and me set off the kids' rockets they'd been building in rocketry. When they're up in the sky I get so paranoid that they're going to land on the kids' heads and hurt them in some horrific way, but Cara just encourages it:
Cara: "10 points if you hit Bud, 50 points for Earl!"

Then the kids run around like crazed dogs, squealing and pleading with their rockets to land near the office for the points.

1:56pm Emily and me were comparing our luscious locks and soft skin earlier. The kids have all these expensive beauty products and just leave them in the shower for the poor counselors to take advantage of – rude not to really.

Loads of the kids have got this 'mono' thing now, although some of them are calling it 'strep'. I'm sure they're just doing it to get out of lessons. Wow, I'm so unsympathetic, I sound like my mum. They don't sound any different though when they talk – they're just moping around more and moaning that it hurts. I'm a non-believer.

7:13pm At meal times we normally have to sit at tables with our bunks, but today they randomly let everyone sit where they wanted. The campers were so confused – it was pretty funny. The girls are always moaning that you have to sit in the same place and then as soon as they're given the opportunity to move and sit wherever, they all stayed put. Proves that people need order and to be told what to do.

In our free Cara and me went down to the waterfront. We played on the canoes, tubes, trampoline and up the iceberg; it was lots of fun. But when we got back to visual arts I saw Ben and the look on his face brought me right down. He'd got mad at one of his kids and ended up punching the bed and splitting the wood. It looked like his knuckles had moved out of place and his hand was swollen and red. If the kid complains he'll definitely get fired. Thinking of him not being here makes me feel sick and weak. I told Ben and it made him cry. I'm pretty sure this shit is because of me. The kid he'd gone crazy at is actually one of Ben's favourites so I know him. I went to check he was ok and he seemed really shaken up by it all. He said Ben's been really weird the past three days – which is how long we haven't been talking – and that he didn't know why Ben had done it. Ben said he'd felt so shit lately and really angry, he just lost it. He didn't directly say it was because of me, but I could tell he was thinking it. I really hope he doesn't get in shit, although he should do.

7:53pm Oh god, I've just been to see Danielle in rest hour as I hadn't seen her for a while. She was by herself sat on her bed in her bunk crying and holding a photo of her mum and brother. She told me how they'd both died in the same month – her mum had breast

cancer and her brother leukaemia. How do you get over that? She said she'd had a really bad day and was really missing them. Puts me having a moan yesterday into perspective. Other people have been through so much in their lives, I'm lucky. Danielle is so much fun and so upbeat all the time. I just thought of her as a hard nut scal who wasn't interested in going to university and was just happy to hang out at home doing random jobs. But she didn't go to university because she was looking after her mum, and when her mum and brother died she decided there was more to life than textbooks.
Danielle: "I miss them both so much."

9:23pm I had to watch yet another shit show tonight. I'm so over them now, I can't imagine ever wanting to see another musical again. Now I'm lying on my bed with two of my girls, Stephanie and Alexa. They are funny, but just don't shut up chatting absolute shit. Hmmmm, I want to see Ben, he looked so forlorn earlier. I really hope that kid doesn't say anything.

1:18am Evening off tonight so I went up to horseback with gay Pete. We took some 'sexy' photos with the whips and hats, just for something to do, and then watched the girls' midnight football training. I was really enjoying hanging out with Pete; I haven't seen him for ages, until he started slating me so much about Ben that is. I guess it was in a harmless way, but I didn't like it and it made me feel protective. Pete can't believe I like him and says I can do better – I hate that phrase. He doesn't even know Ben, I don't think he's actually ever even spoken to him so how can he judge? Then after saying I should do better he went on to say:

1. I was fat
2. I should lose weight
3. I do fuck all in visual arts.

Dickhead.

I did something to Rebecca's supposed best friend Jo earlier and I feel really bad. Sometimes I just don't think and she's well pissed off at me. She finally got it on with the lighting guy last night in the rafters of the Kennedy Theatre near us. I was in her bunk earlier and just casually dropped it into conversation, with all the kids in there. She gave me the filthiest look and shut me up straight away. Then she grabbed my hand and pulled me outside.

Jo: "What I do in my time off and what I talk to the kids about are two different things. I don't want my personal life discussed in front of them."

Oops. My bad.

Monday 25th July

9:30am Loudspeaker: "Eeeeeeeeeeeevvverybody up, up, up! It's time to riiiise and shiiine… It's a beautiful day on the Rockbear campus…"

Woohoo, two-hour lie in for everyone on lazy day! I love being on alternate day staff.

5:57pm I didn't get up until 10:30am and then sunbathed all day with Pip. It's so hot; the girls kept tipping buckets of water on us and running off. It was actually nice to cool down a bit though. The Mean Girls from last session are definitely friendlier now that they've been divided, and they actually seem much happier and more relaxed. I think they're free to have fun now without the pressure of keeping up with each other and the competition of who's best friends with who. Now there's just a core group of five and they've worked out how they can be best friends with each other rather than fighting. It's been a week since the others left and I'm actually enjoying spending time with them. I don't think I could've coped if they'd all stayed on for another three weeks. Last session was awful.

Me, my campers, Pip and her campers all put face packs on and dried them in the sun. That was fun, I felt like I was 12 again, when me and my friends trashed my mum and dad's bathroom with face pack clay all up the walls and over the towels.

After lunch we all boarded the big yellow bus to go to Winkworth cinema to watch *Batman*. I did my usual trick of catching a few zzzs while the film was on. On the way back I sat next to this really sound kid on the bus – he was telling me all about his hopes and aspirations for life. It felt like a very deep conversation to be having with a 14-year-old boy, I can't imagine any boys that age in England being so eloquent.

Little blonde Stephanie has made this hideous looking creature in crafts. It's a piece of foam cut out like a bear and she's painted it orange, given it a few strands of scraggly black wool for hair and drawn a face on it. It's gross, but Stephanie absolutely loves it – I took it off her to look at and she went mental. She carries it everywhere and cuddles up to it at night. It just shows how these kids are so on the 'cusp' of growing up. One day they'll be effing and blinding and talking about sex and boys, then the next they'll just want cuddles and to snuggle and be comforted. It's confusing enough for me.

11:45pm Tonight's evening activity was Brain Wars. Earl divided everyone at the Kennedy Theatre into four equal teams. As a team you nominate a member to go up on stage and answer questions or do forfeits from Bud and Earl for points. It was fun, but trying to control the kids who weren't asked to go up was a nightmare. They were all messing about so Earl decided to deduct some points, which made everyone who did care really angry and war pretty much broke out in my team. To calm it all down they had a singing round where all the kids had to join in and whichever team sang it the best won, easy. They sang Billy Joel's, *Piano Man*. It was really emotional hearing the whole camp singing together – some of the kids were waving their hands in the air like they had lighters and they were putting their arms around each other's shoulders. It was a really lovely moment.

God they work you like dogs up at the horse section. I spoke to Pete after Brain Wars; he fell off a gator the other day and has seriously fucked up his knee. He lifted his trouser leg up to show me and it's really swollen and bruised – it actually looks like the bone is protruding under his skin. The boss of the horses section won't let him take time off to go to see a doctor because they're short-staffed and the camp nurse is just like, "ah you'll be fine". If that were one of the kids we'd have about 10 ambulances here by now.

There's going to be a huge storm tonight – I can see the lightning flashes already from my pink armchair on the porch. I'm just going to sit and watch it and think about what an incredible seven weeks I've had so far.

Tuesday 26th July

12:36pm Woohoo, made it up for running club today! Met up with Emily, had a little run, felt really sick, got the piss taken out of me by some early-rising counselors, felt a bit more sick, came home, and I'm not going again. Hurts too much and I need sleep doing this job. The other 13 people in my bunk weren't too impressed when the alarm woke them up either.

Ben and his camper are friends again so he's not going to get in trouble. He chose a good kid to hassle there; he's mature enough to understand Ben would be thrown out of camp if the head counselors found out, and he doesn't want that. It's not like he hurt the kid or anything, he just scared him. Ben and me are talking again now too. Not properly, but at least we're acknowledging each other. I still need to ask him why the fuck he didn't tell me that he had a girlfriend before though.

2:46pm My favourite camper here is this scrawny little eight-year-old girl from one of the local villages. She's at camp on a scholarship and is just so sweet and loving.
Me: "Are you having fun at camp?"
Her: "Yes... but I don't really have any friends here."
Me: "Aww, I'm sure you have. Why do you say that?"
Her: "No one will talk to me because I'm poor."
This broke my heart.
Her: "I haven't got all the cool stuff everyone else has."

She does look scraggly – she needs a good wash. She said she was having fun by herself, but she was really missing her dad. She's such a little cutie, especially compared to all the horrible spoilt children here. I love her.

Cara and me have started calling all the visual arts staff who came in the second bus load, the second session bitches – it's not good. Think our combined jealousy is making us hate them and we should probably stop it.

4:15pm Ben skived off his lesson to come and find me at my bunk on my free. He did his usual thing of standing outside the side door and shouting my name. My bunk is right by that door, but I tried to hide.
Him: "I know you're in there."
I came out and he launched straight into it.
Him: "Are you and me ok now? It feels like you're being funny with me."
Me: "Why didn't you tell me you had a girlfriend before?"
Him: "You never asked, and she's not important here. We're having fun aren't we? Well we were."

Me: "That's such a horrible thing to say, for me, and her. I really didn't think you were like that. Haven't you even thought about my feelings? And hers?"

We were silent, but my anger was bubbling.

Me: "I can't believe you're planning to go back home and marry a girl you've been cheating on for a month. How can you do that?"

He didn't answer me.

Me: "I just don't understand why you wouldn't tell me from the start."

Him: "I really liked you Lucy. Still like you. We've had so much fun here, and... I just thought... I didn't think it really mattered what was happening back at home. Camp... and you... it just feels like a different world. I don't feel like the same Ben here. When I go home I'll slot back into my old ways, and you will too so don't look at me like that. Life here is just totally different, and I love it. I don't want us to change."

I didn't know what to say. It was nice to hear, but not in the way he'd said it, or in the circumtances.

Him: "We've got five weeks left of being in the same country, of being on the same continent, why don't we just enjoy it for what it is? My girlfriend is my issue to deal with. It's not something you need to worry about. Let's just have fun and enjoy being with each other."

Head counselor: "Everything ok Lucy?"

She was checking the bunks and must've heard our raised voices.

Me: "Yes, sorry, he's just going."

The head counselor and me just looked at him, and he left.

Me: "I'm alright. He's just an idiot, that's all."

7:02pm I just found this note in my bed. I'm in love...

Lucy,
You're so amazing and funny. I'm so glad you're my counselor and I know I'm annoying sometimes, but I don't mean to be. I think you're pretty and really sweet, I just wanted you to know.
Stephanie x

1amish Danielle and me really wanted to get out of camp tonight. Everyone was saying the GC was closed, but no one could actually be bothered to climb the massive hill to check. So Danielle and me met at midnight and snuck off into the woods on camp to have a cigarette. This was incredibly stupid – Earl's first wife died from throat cancer and now if you get caught with a cigarette you're fired, immediately, even if you're off camp. He said he has spies everywhere and he'll know. So yeah, not really sure why Danielle and me felt the need to do it on camp – it was fun though – bit of a buzz, but then we just got sad...

You have to be so upbeat all day at camp. You need to be constantly alert to deal with everything that comes at you and stay strong, kind and yet authoritative towards the kids all day and night. It's easy to feel down in the rare moments when all the buzz and commotion has disappeared. I start thinking deeply about too many things and it's really overwhelming. We talked about how emotional the last few weeks at camp have been – it's been tough, but there's been no time to indulge in those little old things called feelings. It's so hard to stay positive around the kids and not face your own doubts and confidence crises. Since finding out about Danielle and her life the other day, I'm trying not to let myself get down about things, but everything is relative.

We both said we were scared to go home, although for different reasons. She doesn't have university or a job to go back to. She needs to decide what she's going to do with her life and that's a lot to think about. I know exactly what I'll be doing, back to finish my third year at university and back to Sheffield. I'm so excited about the future though. Camp has opened my eyes up to so much more that I could be doing with my life. I don't want to just live in Sheffield and work in boring jobs, climbing the life ladder dictated by society. I want excitement and to travel and really live. Although I moan about everyone and everything, I've never enjoyed life as much as I have being here.

Wednesday 27th July

3:30pm Cara's face when I told her who Taylor Corraddi, David's daughter was, was brilliant. She made a beeline for her and struck up the conversation by telling her how much she just 'loved' her bracelets and what an 'amazing' style she has. Oh, and how 'incredible' her hair is. Then there were some not-so-subtle questions about her house and what it was like, before just blatantly asking if she could come and stay with them. She is one brazen Irish girl, but Taylor wasn't having any of it. She obviously just thought Cara was a weirdo, and she's probably had all this fake praise from all the other counselors already. Life's tough when your dad's an international celebrity.

There are quite a few famous kids here this session actually – I've heard rumours of Portia Smith's* son, Simon Eastwood's* grandchildren and Cara said that Jane Lawson* [more super-famous celebs] used her skanky toilet when there wasn't any toilet roll. Haha, bet they're not used to that. I can't imagine *what* these kids think when they come here from their million dollar Upper East Side Manhattan apartments.

The South African woman up at craft blatantly hates Cara and me. She doesn't trust us with her precious store cupboard one bit. Cara and me are supposed to teach crafts together just the two of us, but she hangs around on her free watching us like a hawk. She's such a bitch too. I know I'm a gossip, but at least I provide some ammunition for everyone else – it should be give and take. Even though she obviously doesn't like Cara and me she slags everyone off to us, including the woman who teaches ceramics who is about her age so I thought they'd be friends. She's got her head stuck so far up her arse I'm not surprised she can't see the kids robbing the sticky glitter from the cupboard.

Keakuki and me were messing around earlier. We were facing each other, holding hands and leaning back. I kept going further and further back.

Me: "If you loved me you wouldn't let me go!"

She was laughing and squealing. I think she loved the attention – I've heard her new counselors are finding her a bit of a handful. Lately, whenever I've seen her wandering around camp, she's been by herself with a scowl on her face. It's obvious she's had enough here. I've never seen her in a play so she's not here for the performing arts; when it comes to the stage I think she's actually really shy.

9:18pm My campers and me just found Zoe's showreel in her stuff after a tip off from Pip. It was so cool. She's been in *Neighbours* and a few Australian adverts, including one for Coca Cola. It was weird to see her on screen, but she looked good!

11:42pm God, trying to get my campers to stay in at night is such a stress sometimes. I have to go calling for them at the doors like they're rogue cats out on the prowl. Pete told one of his to get in last night after he'd taken them out for pizza as a treat for cleaning up the bunk, and the camper replied, "Go shovel shit horse boy".

Thursday 28th July

1:51pm It's *unbelievably* noisy in the canteen at meal times. The boys' tables have an obsession with tapping their spoons in some apparently melodic way, girls sing, counselors shout and plates clatter: it's insane. The campers are bobbing up and down, up and down, and Earl and Bud are shouting at everyone to sit down and eat their meals. Whatever I think about the older kids' canteen time though, it's nothing compared to the young ones. When I go in to see Cara and Emily the food is literally everywhere – faces, floor, walls and clothes – the kids are screaming and the kitchen staff look on traumatised from behind the safety of the serving stations.

Lunch today was chicken wings, perogis and this butternut squash dish that was covered in a layer of marshmallow. No wonder the kids are bouncing off the walls, depressed and fat. Every day they just get high on sugary foods and then sent back down again with drugs.

6:55pm When it comes to guys she likes, Cara falls apart. I was watching her talk to the Polish guy she likes from mountain bikes earlier and she went all giggly and red, tripping on her words. It was very sweet. She just wants to meet a nice man. She says all the guys she's been with in Ireland are dicks who just use her and treat her like shit. She wants to do the yearlong working visa in Australia to get away from them all, but all her friends at home are 'dry shites' who won't go with her and she doesn't want to go by herself. I wish I could sack off the third year of university and go, but I really don't have enough money and mum and dad would go mental. Cara said all her friends at home are only interested in getting married and having babies and she's really bored there. She left her catering job to come here because she hated working every evening and weekend when everyone else was out having fun. I reckon she should sack in all this catering and work with children. She's brilliant with them.

7:46pm I've just been chilling with little bitch Britney on the terrace. I think I'm actually starting to like her, just a bit. I should probably stop referring to her as little bitch Britney. She has a really sneaky sense of humour – a bit filthy, a bit mean, but very funny. She was taking the piss out of all the campers going past with 'vocal rest' signs hung around their necks and doing silly impressions of them. She was making me laugh, a lot.

9:12pm We had a party in the bunk for one of my campers' birthdays earlier. We pulled the mattresses off all the beds and lay them out in the middle to lie on. Now the ice cream is somehow smeared over everything and the girls are all lying on the mattresses with their trouser buttons open. They're filled with food regret from the eight tubs of Ben & Jerry's we've just scoffed and they're blaming me, jut screaming 'Luucccyy' at the top of her voice.

There's this girl in Pip's bunk who all the girls take the piss out of. She's horrible to them too though, so I don't feel that sorry for her. She walks, talks and dresses like a boy, so the kids are always saying she's a lezza. Sometimes she's like, 'yeah and what,' then other times she gets really upset. Of course I don't really care either way, but it's interesting watching how the kids react to each other and predicting what their life will turn out like based on my friends. I'm not judging them; I'm just thinking how I used to be a loud-mouthed, cocky bitch when inside I always felt really insecure and hated myself. Obviously now I know that being loud and annoying is quite standard for someone who's insecure, and my teachers must've known this. They could see what was really going on in my head and probably made assumptions about my life too. I'm just applying the anthropology and sociology I've learnt over the years to them and most probably stereotyping.

She must get absolutely ripped at school, and she'll spend a lot of her life defending herself. At the moment it's obvious she's having trouble accepting who she is, but so do most teenagers I guess. She's a fun and silly person – I've had her in my lessons and she's a good laugh – but she's also very angry. She has these epic rages where she just goes mental at everyone and tries to smash the bunk up. Pip's got her work cut out there.

11:23pm Cara and me hung out with the boys in rock shop in our free today. We pretended we were rock stars and smashed the drums and took cool photos of us with the guitars. I've always wanted to be able to play the guitar – never got round to it – any child of mine will learn though. I love it at rock shop – there's a recording studio and it's where all the cool kids hang out. The counselors are all really fit in there too. Things between me and Tim – the guy I snogged in the first week – are cool. He's actually really funny and is getting with one of the girls from tennis now.

You can tell Cara feels intimidated by the girls here. I think it's hard for her to speak up for herself when she's in a group. I find everything Cara says funny, which is probably why she likes me so much. If we're not together people will ask me where Cara is, and vice versa. Rebecca made some bitchy comment about us boxing ourselves off and excluding everyone else the other day. Well whatever, she's doing that by being constantly miserable and only ever talking to the girl from the kitchen in corners in whispers. It's so important to have good friends at camp and Cara is the most fun person to hang out with here. It annoys me that people won't take the time to get to know her and give her a chance.

Stephanie's tooth came out today so the head counselor gave me a few quarters to put under her pillow. Now the big challenge is getting them there, I don't want her to wake up with my ugly face hanging over hers or she'd be traumatised for life. I'm thinking of dropping in *Mission Impossible* style – might be a bit drastic though.

11:40pm Mission accomplished. I held my breath and crept over on tippy toes while trying not to laugh. I managed to slip it under her pillow with just the smallest murmur from her. I had to go outside afterwards to deep breathe. That was funny, now I can add 'tooth fairy' to my CV too.

Friday 29th July

8:13pm Day off today. I went to Ithaca with the other alternate dayers. Pete and me had breakfast at an organic restaurant and then explored Ithaca and the Pyramid Shopping Mall. We went on a bus ride around Cornell University, which is one of the Ivy Leagues along with Yale and Stanford. We saw all the frat houses with the Greek lettering out the front and students walking around clutching folders. It was so perfectly kept and all the buildings were incredible. My university definitely doesn't look like that!

I agreed to get Stephanie and Alexa some Cup Noodles because they've decided they won't eat the camp food and want to be like Britney and her crew. Now I've ended up with about 20 things on my Walmart shopping list from the rest of the kids. They were all saying they'd give me money to get them what they want. I'll do it for them for free, this time. It must be weird for them not going anywhere but camp for three weeks, sometimes even six. They were all over me when I came back with the supplies. If I'd have known in session two that all it took was a Cup Noodle to make them love me, I would've come with a tray full.

Saturday 30th July

1:50pm Stephanie has been unusually quiet today so I went and sat with her on her bunk when we got back from lunch. The past two days she's been in bed at every opportunity and not really talking, so I've been a bit worried. When I sat next to her I heard a weird chirping noise – she looked at me guiltily and cast her eyes to her side under the cover – I looked where her eyes were pointing and discovered a little injured bird. She'd found it outside and wanted to keep it – she is *so* cute. I could tell she was in love with it, but I was horrified. I hate birds and creatures, especially when they come on human property. They give me the creeps. I took it off her and she was crying and desperately pleading with me to allow her to keep it. I felt *so* mean. We can't have it in the bunk though; it's probably disease-ridden for starters. I can't believe she's had it in her bed, eugh. I gave it to the head counselor and I presume she killed it. Stephanie was so upset; I don't think she'll ever talk to me again.

7:20pm Cara and me have been trying to get the Polish guy she likes from mountain bikes to take us out on a bike trip all summer. Today was our day. He actually came and found us. We got fitted for a bike and followed him up into the mountains. I've never been mountain biking before, over rocks and up and down hills. It was so hard and scary as he was going so fast, but it was lots of fun. I spent most of my childhood riding around my village, but I was always scared of going up and down pavements, so the rocky mountain paths were terrifying. We tried to keep up with him, but he was obviously trying to wear us out. He turned to see where we were and the corners of his mouth rose to a sadistic smile when he saw we were struggling. Freewheeling down the huge hills was incredible – I felt so free and amazing. The mountain air was brilliantly fresh and I was so focused I forgot all about camp while we were up there.

We were so sweaty by the time we got back. Cara decided to start a water fight with the Polish guy – she was definitely doing the whole flirty squealing girl thing. She's so into him it's funny, although she does seem to be into any semi-fit guy that moves these days. I hope he takes us out again sometime and that we haven't ruined our chances by managing to keep up. We made him a thank you card in our crafts lesson to suck up anyway.

7:52pm Kind of got back with Ben today. Not that we ever finished, or even started, but I guess it's been on hold for the nine days since he told me he had a frikkin girlfriend. We were blatantly flirting all day – it was super fun. No kids came to radio so I skived off to use the computers. He was in there with some counselor laid on the bench next to him and as I walked past him I ran my fingers down his back. He got up straight away and came and sat next to me, leaving her lying there. Woo yeah! She came and sat next to us, but he totally ignored her.

My new plan of action is to chill out and just enjoy being with him for the next four weeks. I'm not going to obsess, expect or want anything too serious, but just enjoy us as we are. He seems to be all I've thought about for the past few days and it's literally driving me crazy.

Every department within visual arts has a specially decorated t-shirt for the counselors except for rocketry, so Ben designed a wicked one for us. That's got to mean something.

Only one week left of this session and it's goodbye Mean Girls! Yes ahhh!

Sunday 31st July

10:45am Another lazy day, woo yeah! Rebecca, Zoe, Cara and all the other normal-day counselors went on their day off earlier to Ithaca, while us alternate-day staff were left guarding the kids. Earl and Bud decided to make it a proper lazy day this time though, where we don't actually do *anything*. Ahh, Rebecca's going to be screwing, she's so annoyed she wasn't chosen to be on alternate day this year. I cleaned up the bunk earlier for something to do and found $20 down the back of the bed – jackpot. Then I went to sleep for three hours, while the kids did their own thing in the bunk. Now I'm sitting in and watching the storm from the comfort of Britney's armchair on the terrace. I *love* being on alternate day.

2:16pm The kids are menacing me, but it's actually pretty funny. Today as I was showering they decided it would be hilarious to pour bottles of freezing cold water over the top of the cubicle onto me. I was hamming it up how annoyed I was and they were laughing and squealing. I need to think of something good to get them back for that. I have to be careful though – there's no way I could do the same – imagine if they told Earl I'd been pouring cold water on them as they showered, he would *not* find it funny.

7:16pm It's been so nice to have a day away from Rebecca. She's absolutely doing my head in. The guy from tennis she'd been going out with for like a week finished with her and it's all she fucking talks about. BORING. It's either that, or her trip to Puerto Rico with the girl she's always whispering with from the kitchen, the little kids' head counselor – the one with the scary eyebrows – and some other counselor from visual arts that she blatantly invited to make up the numbers. She seems set on making me jealous about it for some reason, but I really couldn't give a shit. She asked me if I wanted to go, I said no, so I don't know why she feels the need to pummel every last little detail into me. Emily said she was going on about it to her too at the staff meeting the other night – she's *so* self-obsessed! She doesn't listen to a thing anyone else says and she makes everything all about her, all the time. She's also turning out to be a surprise rival for Zoe in the worst skiver stakes. I swear I've done all the work this session.

Zoe, jeez, I can't even think about her without getting irate. As her co-counselor, I can't stand her. She's absolutely fucking useless. She's more work than help and one of the most irritating and annoying people I've ever met. She struts around with her scraggy bleached hair pouting and preening and flashing her dodgy fake tan job. I wish she'd stop trying to skank off the kids too – she compliments them on something and they'll obviously say thanks and then she'll be like, "Can I have it?" Emily says in Australia they'd call her a 'bogan' – I guess that's their version of a 'pikey'.

God, I sound like a bitch, but this is five weeks of finding Zoe unbelievably annoying and eight weeks of Rebecca. I'm proud of myself for putting up with them both for so long; I would've thought I'd have gone crazy by now. I need to try and only be with them when I really have to be and ignore or block them at every available opportunity if I'm going to get through the next four weeks without going insane.

Cara hates Rebecca; actually I think she hates anyone who's serious more than 10 per cent of the time. I have had some in-depth and somber chats with Cara, but her aim in life is to have fun. A good aim if you ask me. She doesn't enjoy moping around like a lot of other people do, Rebecca for example. A lot of the other counselors have the wrong impression of her – she's not just some Irish airhead who likes pink things and messing around. I hate seeing her just sweeping up when she should be working with the kids in the second-session bitches' lessons. She won't stand up for herself and now she's got her iPod she's happy enough sweeping and singing away, but it makes me sad. She's better with the children than any of them and she shouldn't be made to feel like the only way she can contribute is by sweeping up. Fucking dry shites pissing me right off.

Too much time to think today! I think I'm going a bit insane. I feel like Holden Caulfield from *Catcher In The Rye*. Maybe it's cabin fever from staying in all day.

Monday 1st August

4:09pm I know the South African witch up at visual arts thinks Cara and me are shit, but I actually think she's the shit one. She asked the visual arts boss if she could officially help in mine and Cara's crafts class and all she does now is man the store cupboard, Hitler-style. She lets the kids have just one colour pen at a time, and one piece of card – tight bitch. She knows more about craft than we do so could actually teach something, but you can tell she prefers the petty power of dishing out pipe cleaners. I actually think she hates the kids too. I've never seen her have a laugh or joke with them, she just has this permanent look of disapproval on her face – why is she even here? I'm not surprised she finds us annoying; she should be sat at home tending to her pot plants at her age.

7:13pm One of the campers here – who seems to have taken a liking to me – has some sort of weird disease. Her skin is all scaly, she's all juddery, her eyes are oozing and she's all phlegmy. I think she has some degree of Asperger's Syndrome too. Cara says she can't go near her and 'admires' me for being able to hug her and be close to her. She's so queasy when the kids are a bit gross. She's got this camper with black, wiry, long, scraggly hair and there's always thick hair everywhere in her bunk. Emily brushed it for her the other day and Cara said she thought she was going to be sick with all the thick hairs gathering on the floor. She was actually heaving when she was trying to tell me about it. A few weeks ago I was like Cara, queasy at the thought of touching gross kids, but after cleaning that bunk day in day out and all the hugs I've had to give out to dirty children this summer my standards have slipped as low as they'll go. I really don't care anymore.

Anyway, this girl keeps tracking me down around camp and wanting to hug me. She makes me cards and presents up at visual arts. She's another one who really wants to go home and I think she thinks I can help in some way. Her head counselor told me she's not going anywhere though, her parents have said she has to stay until the end. It's probably cheaper for her parents to send her here for the summer rather than to get specialist care for her.

9:49pm Zoe has just gone absolutely psycho at the kids.
Zoe: "Who the *fuck* has eaten my chocolate Tim Tams? My mum sent those from Australia especially. I'm not going to see her for ages. Don't you have your own candy for fuck's sake? I hope whoever did it feels really bad right now."
I do Zoe, I really do.

Tuesday 2nd August

8:09am I swear, just the littlest thing can drive you crazy at camp. I'm tired and irritable I know, but I really hate the way Rebecca thumps across the bunk in the morning not picking her feet up. She makes like a scuff-thump, scuff-thump noise as she goes, and I have to grit my teeth to stop myself flipping out.

7:09pm Oops, got another bollocking down at waterfront on my break. The little kids, Cara's kids, were asking me to chuck them in the water from the pier. I was merrily going along lobbing them in while feeling the head lifeguard's eagle eye on me. Then it came to Sally, now she's a big girl, not fat, just looks about 12 rather than seven. I couldn't lift her properly and didn't have her in a very good grip so I kind of dropped her/kind of threw her in. Her nose was about an inch from the edge of the metal pier. My heart was racing. The head lifeguard shouted at me from the beach for being so stupid and then one of the other lifeguards came to tell me off too. I had to be like, "Yah whatever, she was fine," and turn away. You could probably see how shaken up I was from my face though. Sally got out, ran back around and asked me to do it again. I took the incident as my cue to leave, but what a trooper.

9:19pm Awww, just seen one of my cute rocketry kids up at canteen. He's well excited for Cara and me to meet his mum and dad on parents' day. He's got such a lovely smile and I love his blonde bowl cut – he should be a Hollywood child star. Love him. Hmmm, I wonder if his parents are famous?

Ben and me are back on track. Had a 'great' time up in the roller rink last night. Ar yes.

Wednesday 3rd August

9:20am Whenever it's anyone's birthday at camp they get a cake brought out to them at breakfast and everyone in the dining hall has to sing Happy Birthday. It must be weird to have your birthday at camp and not see your family and friends. Some kids have been coming to camp since they were seven – when you think about it, they could've spent 10 years having birthdays at camp, not sharing it with their friends and family. That's mad.

1:55pm There's a phantom shitter at camp. One of the boys poos in the middle of his bunk and just leaves it there to fester. Cara and me found a pile on the floor of the portaloo near the art department earlier too. We're on a mission to find out who it is.

7:16pm Cara and me managed to persuade the Polish mountain bike guy to let us out on the bikes by ourselves today. We tried to follow the route he'd taken us before, but obviously being us we got totally lost. It was really scary not knowing where we were up on the mountains. All the paths, trees and rocks looked the same. We knew we had to get back down, but then we wouldn't be able to see where the camp was so we had to be sure before we started the descent. It was the first time we'd been out by ourselves for eight weeks and no one knew where we were either. It was only the Polish guy who knew we'd left camp, and he probably shouldn't have let us so wouldn't raise an alarm until next week, maybe. Cara was terrified a bear was going to eat us. After taking a few wrong turns and being absolutely shit scared we finally found the Camp Rockbear sign. The joy and relief I felt at seeing that was beautiful. I had *The Sign* by Ace of Base going around in my head. We ended up being about 20 minutes late for the leather class we were meant to be teaching though and the visual arts boss was raging. Bitch, we've had a traumatic time, she should be comforting us.

9:02pm The rock shop staff put on a rock festival tonight for the evening activity. It was very sweet, but sounded absolutely awful. The kids were all playing their own songs that they'd worked on this summer on the 'main stage' and there was another 'acoustic stage' round the back of the rock shop. I just used it as an opportunity to have a lie down on the grass while all the other counselors watched the kids. I was thinking about Ben. I don't know what I'm doing just letting him off the hook. I'm not sure it's right morally – but then we're having so much fun now we're back together. If we'd have been in the real world there's no way I would've let him get away with it, but we're thousands of miles away from home. Why should his girlfriend matter to me here? I feel guilty, but that's his issue to deal with, I think.

Thursday 4th August

2:02pm I haven't felt very well at all today – think it was from the excessive drinking last night. We went around the lake and I drank so much it was ridiculous. As always, it was a *lot* of fun. We had a fire going and a good little group and I really enjoyed chatting to some of the counselors who came in the second innings. They're actually pretty funny, hmmm maybe I should have given them more of a chance before writing them off as 'second-session bitches'. All the counselors started partying round there now – there are too many bad associations with the GC to really enjoy a night there. When Earl closed it after the accident I think he unintentionally made it responsible. If we go round the lake driver John goes into Winkworth and gets the booze for us and it's only 50 cents a can, so it's cheaper than the GC too.

I wish me and Cara had the same day off – she tried to get Emily to swap so we could go to Six Flags together, I knew there was no chance. Ben wanted me to swap with Rebecca or Zoe so we could have a day off together too. Fuck that – it means you miss out on two days off together, not worth it!

That girl I decided has Asperger's is driving the head counselors insane. She needs permanent one to one help and attention and can't be trusted by herself. It's not really fair on the other campers that she's here – she takes up all the counselors' time. I don't know whose bunk she's in, but I feel sorry for them. The head counselor brings her up to me because they've had enough, but it's hard to look after her while looking after all the other kids too.

Cara told me about her older sister today, she'd never mentioned her before. She said she's never felt like she could match up to her, because she's apparently so beautiful and intelligent and Cara's always felt like shit in her shadow. She's an archeologist with a nice boyfriend and a house in the country. When I was growing up I always wanted a sister, but I don't think I could've coped with the jealousy, it must be hard. I think Cara is amazing, I can't imagine a better version. She was genuinely sad when she was telling me about growing up though. She's always felt like the black sheep of the family because she goes out drinking and getting with boys and her sister never did anything naughty. Her family treat her like some kind of goddess and Cara's just desperate to do something to really make them proud of her.

8:19pm When we went on our bike ride around the lake the other day I noticed this big, scary, empty house. I told my campers about it and they've been begging me to take them ever since. I told Pip about it earlier so she rounded up the kids and we went on a mission. Alexa and Stephanie came with us, and Britney dragged a few of her followers along. We walked around the lake and told them some scary stories involving bears tramps and campers. A tree

had fallen down and was blocking the path – Pip told the kids it happened when a camper ran off and climbed it. The bears pawed at it to try and get the child, making it weaken and fall down.
Pip: "We never did see that camper again."
Britney screamed. Haha they can't believe that, surely? They were shaken up, but we carried on a bit further. I turned around suddenly and shouted 'boo' at them. They absolutely shit themselves and were all holding onto each other squealing.
Pip: "Are ya wussies? Ya wanna go back?"

They were pleading to carry on. It was rest hour so it was getting pretty dark; I was spooked, but obviously didn't want to show it. We found this little hut and all went in. There was a closed fridge in there.
Me: "Shall I open it?"
Pip: "What if there's a dead body in there?"

The girls were shitting it. If they weren't making me laugh so much with how scared they were, I would've been too. I went to open it, then looked back at them dramatically, then opened it properly and screamed loudly. The girls all ran out screeching – obviously there was nothing there, comedy gold though.

We carried on running up the road for a bit until we came to the house we'd come to see. It was one of those typical wooden American houses, but all the windows had been smashed in and the paint was peeling off. Trees surrounded it and there was a little path leading up to the door. I went at the front and Pip at the back and we had the girls in the middle. I took it slowly, but nearly put my foot through the bottom doorstep. It was at this point that I realised I didn't actually know how many girls had come with us and no one at camp knew where we were. We were less than a mile away, but we didn't know the camp phone number, or even have a mobile on us. We carried on anyway and slowly made our way into the house. I stood in the front room and looked round. The wind whistled through the broken windows as I clocked the sleeping bag in the corner next to a small table holding a gas lamp and a few bits of half-eaten food. We were all silently taking it in then suddenly we heard a creak and a cough from upstairs. Oh my god, I *absolutely* shit myself.
Me: "Run!"

We legged it laughing and screaming back to camp around the lake. The girls kept jumping up and down and holding onto each other in delight and fear. Pip and me just looked at each other, wondering what the fuck we were both thinking going down there.

When we got back the head counselor was waiting on our porch for us. The campers were hyper and blurted out what we'd just done before running off to tell their friends. Thankfully, she seemed to find it funny. She just said not to do it again without telling her or another head counselor so they know where the campers are at all times. I for one definitely won't.

8:45pm I tried to email my friends at home earlier to tell them about my adventures, but I just feel a million miles away from them, physically and mentally. All the things that have happened to me this summer, all the incredible people I've met and the amazing experiences I've had, they don't know any of it. I'm living in a completely different world. I did email them, but nothing of any interest. Everything is the same for them. It's troubling me that I feel so distant. I can't imagine what it's going to be like when I go back, I feel like I've changed so much.

The computer room is set out in two long aisles – four rows of computers with the ones in the middle facing each other. While I was in there earlier two kids tap danced their way up and down the aisles singing some song from the *Blood Brothers* play we had to endure the other night. It was very funny, but the geek that runs the IT room didn't think so. His face was going red he was shouting at them so much to stop it. I left him to it and went to find Cara.

10:38pm Pip and her campers from next door brought their mattresses into our bunk earlier. We set them all on the floor and had a card game marathon. We played sevens and rummy and they taught me some new games I don't remember the names of. It was so fun and what I imagined camp to be like when I originally applied to come – it probably is at girls' camps and scout camps, but these kids aren't innocent enough for this every night. They'd prefer to be out eyeing up boys and dancing around to Pussycat Dolls.

1:06am Had another midnight meeting tonight, which went something like...

Earl: "The campers are having a brilliant time and the shows are going well. You're all doing brilliantly. It's been a long summer and I know you're all very tired now, but we need to work as team and keep on going. There's just three weeks left, let's make them great."

He just carried on about the next lot of kids coming, how they deserve to have as much fun as the first session kids and so we need to stay on our toes and keep the energy and enthusiasm up. I actually feel like I need to sleep for a week.

Friday 5th August

8:57am Emily and me decided to go for a long walk this morning before wake up, seeing as I'm shit at running and too lazy first thing. We walked around the lake and there was this beautiful mist settled over it, I wish I'd bought my new camera. As we passed the swimming pool we saw two deer. They stood perfectly still and proud and stared right at us. We did the same. It lasted about a minute then they ran off, it was a really beautiful moment.

We talked about Ben and the other boys at camp. I love having a bit of a bitch with Emily and it's great to feel like you're away from camp, even if it is just for a few minutes and a few metres away. Emily's really into this guy who works on the climbing wall with her, but he's going out with this trashy girl from visual arts. The one Rebecca is going on holiday with. I can't *believe* he's into her. If I were a guy she'd be one of the last girls I'd go for. She's got long, skanky, straggly hair and she could easily pass for 40. Apparently last session, the time when I was wrecked and they all got MaccyDs and I didn't realise, Emily thought the girl was some local tramp that one of the guys had picked up in the bar. She was trying to get her out of the car and kept telling her she couldn't come back to camp if she wasn't a counselor. Ah, wish I'd been awake for that.

11am If my period doesn't come in the next few days I will shit myself. I really can't work out when my last one was. Fuck. Fuck. Fuck. I do not want a little Ben-shaped baby.

7:18pm God, Rebecca and her little friend from the kitchen are so annoying. I know I'm only finding them so annoying because I'm nosy and want to know what they're talking about, but still. They sit by Rebecca's bed whispering and have all these secret codes. I swear they make each other depressed – they're both right mardy sods these days. I think they're bitching about boys – both of them are taking their camp relationships *way* too seriously.

Since me and Pip took the kids round the lake campers come up to us every day asking when the next trip to see the crazy guy's house is. There's *no* way I'm going near that place again – especially not with kids in tow.

I was watching Ben earlier and just thinking how we would *not* be together in the real world. He's so soft and hippy-like. As much as I'm into him at camp and he's a lot of fun to be around, I don't think I really take him seriously. He's so cringey. I'd be embarrassed to introduce him to mum and dad. I'm too practical and matter-of-fact to get his spirituality. I'd like to, but I just don't really believe in it. Actually, I believe in the mind reading – I've seen that in action. But then I also believe you can be so in tune with someone that you can roughly predict what they're going to say. Oh I don't know. Could be true, could not, at least it's interesting I guess. Emily thinks it's all bullshit – she doesn't like him.

Ben told me earlier how some of the guy counselors have got with the campers this summer. I really can't believe that, ewww the campers seem so young. I guess I am only two years older than some of them, but still, eugh. Apparently it happens loads; Earl would literally go insane if he found out.

9:23pm One more night of the Mean Girls to go! We have to watch so many plays at the end of each session; they're getting boring now. The head counselors round us up to go to the unpopular ones so the kids have an audience. It's the end of the session so the kids have obviously got a million more fun things to be doing – snogging in the bushes, swapping MySpaces and stacking up the Mountain Dew cans probably – so the counselors have to fill the seats.

Me, Rebecca and Zoe had a party in the bunk earlier for the kids leaving. The girls were all telling each other how much they fun they'd had and how much they loved each other – think they were hamming it up a bit, but it was nice to hear.

Saturday 6th August

12:13pm Ooh didn't realise the old South African bitch from crafts was one of the head counselors' mums! That could have all gone very wrong.

Changeover day today. I've just been speaking with my dickhead ex-boyfriend on MSN and he told me about getting with some girl at Chicago Rock back home. Just hearing those words 'Chicago Rock' made me shudder. We are so over – he's scum. Eugh, he makes me sick. I need a nice worldly man who has something more in his life than beer and football. I still need to go home looking really hot though, and then blank him obviously.

Oh. My. God. David Corraddi* is stood outside my cabin leaning against the steps. He's wearing all black, looks really skinny and is just stood there, posing with his Ray-Bans on. The head counselor has strictly forbidden us to talk to him. Zoe just strutted past him flicking her hair and blew him a kiss. Argh, I really want to go and talk to him! Or get a photo at least. I feel this could be one of my biggest life regrets, but I don't want to get chucked out of camp just for hassling him.

2:02pm I'm really enjoying hanging out with Ben normally again. I think I took our whole relationship far too seriously and I was making it more than it is. For about a week I think I felt like I loved him – especially when he took me out on that boat ride, the fucker. I was really dreading the thought of saying goodbye to him, but finding out about his girlfriend has definitely made it easier. I was devastated at the time, but now we're just having lots of fun together. It was a bad time of the month for me I think. Oh and my period came today too, no little Ben baby for me, woohoo!

Rebecca seems so detached from the kids; it's weird. The last days are always a bit manic and because her friend from the kitchen has her own private bunk she skives off in there. I find it odd that she doesn't even want to say bye to the kids. After six weeks, even if you don't like them that much, you definitely have *some* sort of relationship.

3:30pm One of the campers bought her grandad to meet me today...
Camper: "Grandad, come meet my favourite counselor Lucy!"
Me: "Hello sir, ooh I'll be sad to see her go. We've had a great summer together."
Camper: "Lucy's so nice and funny, she's the best."
Grandad: "Where are you from then Lucy, Bryony's quite taken with you."

Me: "Awww, she's great too. I'm from Sheffield, in England."
Cara: "Haha, why are you saying that?"
Me: "Err, because I am?"
Cara: "You're from Australia, aren't you?"
Errrrmmm.

I pointed out that I was in the English team on Independence Day, reminded her about Ben trying to throw me in the lake, and it was only when I asked a passing Pip that Cara believed I was from England. We've been hanging out *every* day for about nine weeks; I can't believe she thought I was from Australia.
Cara: "But you've got blonde hair, and your clothes?"
Haha, she can be *so* thick sometimes.

Cara and me were a bit bored after spending the day sucking up to the kids' parents at the end-of-session art show. The visual arts boss had put loads of food and drink out for them and obviously all the sweets, crisps and chocolate had long gone with all these fatty Americans, but there was about half a watermelon left. Cara challenged me to see who could eat the most. We scoffed it so fast. I looked over at Cara shoveling it in her mouth and we both burst out laughing. Watermelon shot from her nose and landed right on one of the kids' woodwork projects, which made it even funnier. I couldn't swallow the watermelon already in my mouth and snorted instead, which set Cara off again. She was almost choking. Then Ben came in which made us laugh even more. I'm sure he was absolutely disgusted.

It's so weird meeting the parents after looking after their kids for so long. The kids change when their families are about. They generally either completely ignore you as they don't need your support any more, or they really suck up to you. I think with girls it's a power thing – they either treat me like shit, or their parents – to prove some sort of point to the other.

9:17pm Watched a bit of the *Oliver* matinee – just realised there are around 15 shows every session – no wonder I'm sick of them. I probably have to watch about 10 of them each time. After that Cara and me had to launch rockets for the parents. I was responsible for crowd control while she set the rockets up. She had to light the dynamite and use the remote controlled box in her hand to make them launch. All except the last one worked and the parents loved it. She did nearly blow her face off at one point though, but apart from that: a success!

Bowlcut boy came, but his mum and dad never did. My heart bleeds for him. He's the cutest, loveliest kid ever and just wanted to show his mum and dad what he'd been doing for the summer. They'll just send him home with driver John. The rocketry kids are definitely one of my favourite things about camp – they're all so cute and loving. The kid who played Bill Sykes in *Oliver* came along and he was hiding behind me because he was scared of the rockets. How can he be scared of the rockets and then stand up in front of all those people and be so amazing?

I managed to get a spot at the dance show today. It's one of the hottest shows on camp and is always absolutely rammed on changeover day. I felt bad for the dancers though – after the parents had seen their precious little cherub's cha cha across the stage they left. So when it was the next kids' turn they'd come on to see loads of people getting up and going. I'm sure that would never happen in England. Have some respect bitches!

Session Four

Sunday 7th August

7:22pm The new kids arrived last night, they're so cute and sweet I love them already. They're either here by themselves or with just one friend so there are no gangs or groups, and it's the first year at camp for most of them, so no reputations to keep up either. There are only eight girls and they actually seem like they're as good as best friends already. After three practice sessions it was pretty easy to get them settled into the bunk and to get all their clothes and photos set out how they want. They've barely got anything compared to the pink décor of the last six weeks – I was starting to get used to it. It's so spacious in here now with just 11 out of the 16 beds being used – this session should be easy.

These kids are really into the shows as well, which is always good. It gives them something to focus on – and it keeps them out of the bunk in the day because they have so many rehearsals. They already know all the plays and shows that have been marked for this session and have learnt the lines to improve their chances of being cast. They all went off together to join the long audition lines, so I was left in the bunk to chill out and indulge in a little hair wash and shower session. This is what being a camp counselor should be like.

We've got a super counselor this session for the first time too. Super counselors are campers who've been coming here for a few years and now that they're 17 they get a reduced price in return for taking on some counseling duties. It's like they're 'in training' to be counselors next year. Our super counselor had a meeting with all the other supers last night and brought us back pizza. What an angel! I'm so happy I've got a good group of girls to end my camp experience with.

I *really* enjoyed saying bye to the last lot yesterday. I managed to blag loads of stuff off them – clothes, drawers, make up, jewellery – I was right in there. I deserve it too, I can't believe they didn't give me any tips this time. I thought their parents would at least give us the same as they did at the end of second session. Tight fuckers. The key to getting loads of tips is having the parents actually come and pick them up, rather than them just being put on a flight home. This guilt trips them into giving you some cash.

I didn't see Zoe at all in the day yesterday, or Rebecca. I don't know where they went, but I had to get the new campers settled in and talk to all the paranoid parents by myself. I had fun, but it's just annoying when you're the one doing all the work.

11:17pm Just found these letters under my pillow:

"Lucy, I'm going to miss you. I love you sooo much I hope you come back next year. Come to Miami you're going to get raped in Mexico!
<3 always Stephanie"

"Lucy,
I love you, I'm gonna miss you so much. Please KIT you're an amazing counselor! <3 always Alexa"

Aww, I'm going to miss those girls. Love them. Took me a while to work out Keep In Touch, but I think I'm starting to get to grips with all the kids' crazy acronyms after nine weeks.

Monday 8th August

8pm Went to Six Flags Magic Mountain theme park today with all the other alternate dayers. I thought I loved theme parks; I used to go to Alton Towers a few times a year, but I must be getting old. I was on the first ride and the shoulder restraint came down before I was ready. It hit me on the head hard, giving me an instant headache, then after getting chucked about on the ride I realised they just weren't as fun as they used to be. My head hurt for the rest of the day and I just got annoyed with getting thrown about on the rides all day. God, I'm old.

The fact that I'm absolutely knackered didn't help either. Nothing prepared me for how completely and utterly exhausting camp is. I'm working all day and evening, and when it is time to go to bed I just can't switch off. With so many people trying to sleep in one bunk there are always random noises – creaking, snoring, talking, murmuring, muttering – it never ends. Even if you do manage to drift off, you always have to get up again at seven and be bright and sparky, ready for a day of teaching. All day I'm out in the fresh air, eating fat carby food and on my days and evenings off

I'm boozing and trying to make the most of it, doing everything I can. There's just no time to relax. We have rest hour, but you never use it for rest. I like to email or phone home, hang out with Cara or Ben, or just get a shower, and you always have to be around for the kids anyway. I could try to sleep on my hour off too, but by the time you've managed to kick the kids out of the bunk who aren't supposed to be in there it's even shorter. From start to finish, days at camp are absolutely exhausting and it's catching up with me.

I hate to admit it, but I've missed Ben so much today. I was glad to get back to camp. It's weird when you miss the first day of the new kids too. Counselors should be there for the settling in period; otherwise it's harder to get to know them later.

We've got this girl in the bunk who's allergic to gluten, but apparently likes to eat it, so we need to keep an eye on her at mealtimes. The head counselor also told us that the mum of one of our campers is dying of cancer and so she's been sent to camp for some respite. We need to keep an extra eye on her to check she's ok if she ever seems a bit withdrawn or quiet. Poor girl, must be awful for her.

Tuesday 9th August

3:33pm The kids are all getting along really well. They were so enthusiastic about doing clean up this morning; it was great. All I had to do was tell them what to do from the comfort of my bed, and they did it. Not had that happen before!

7:12pm That girl with Asperger's is really annoying. She's started saying I'm being mean to her and screams, "Lucy's horrible" to anyone who will listen in the middle of camp. The head counselor told me not to worry, but it's really pissed me off how I've put myself out to be nice when other counselors and campers ignored her, and then she's doing this to me in return. I know it's something to do with her illness – she wants permanent attention, but I just worry what other people will think hearing her shouting that – especially if she does it when Earl and Bud are around.

8:15pm I've met some amazing people here, but this experience has also made me realise just how fucked up everyone is. No one's life is straightforward, but it's how you deal with the shit that makes the difference. People I admired when I first came here for how chatty, perky, friendly and seemingly fun they are have just turned out to be nuts or on anti-depressants – they can't cope with normal life. Zoe tries to mask her bulimia with her 'zany' craziness, Rebecca's constantly miserable and brings her depressed sister into every conversation possible, Ben's got a psycho side that comes out when life's not going his way and then you look at Danielle. She's been through so much and is still laughing; she's an inspiration, as are some of the campers. In particular I was thinking about some of the kids whose parents died in 9/11. We generally know which ones they are, but they all still laugh and play and have fun like all the other kids. They must have been through so much. There's also this girl who has to wear a full body brace every day. She wears it, deals with it and just gets on with enjoying life. She's a popular kid here and gets good parts in the shows. She doesn't mope about the bunk feeling sorry for herself like some of the other campers do.

Danielle has been through so much, but having a dead mum and brother is not what defines her. I remember at the beginning of camp thinking it weird that what university you went to and where you were from was so important to everyone when you were introducing yourself, but you can allow any part of your life to represent you. What represents Danielle to me is laughter and silliness – in contrast to Rebecca who everyone just thinks is a mardy bitch because that's the part of her personality she shows. She's destined to a life of misery if she's going to let her sister's depression do this to her.

I wonder what my fuck up is? I know that I'm quite extreme. Ben's says it amazes him how peaceful I can be one minute, then crazy and loud the next – he reckons it's because I'm a Libra. I definitely find it hard to be myself sometimes and I act differently around different people, but doesn't everyone?

Being with Ben has been amazing; no guy has ever been so nice to me. I guess that's if I forget the little fact he already has a girlfriend, of course. Our relationship has definitely helped me see what I want in a guy in the future. I want someone I can trust entirely with anything and talk about every subject in the world to. It's helped loads that I always feel like he can read my mind, I've never been very good at saying how I feel, it's great to have him coach it out of me.

I love my friends at home so much, but all of us have screwed each other over at some point during the last eight years. If there's one thing I admire about these American girls, it's how they treat each other. They're so honest about everything and blatantly say if they're annoyed. My friends and me used to go for months without talking to each other, the reason why would be forgotten, but it'd always be over something stupid. These girls argue like sisters, because they know they're best friends. Life would be so much easier for me if I actually said when someone annoyed or hurt me; rather than just gritting my teeth. I can't believe I've lasted so long and intensely with some of the people here, but I've definitely become more accepting and open-minded. Cara and me have spent so much time together in what can often be stressful situations, yet she hasn't annoyed me once. That's never happened before – she's a friend for life.

Wednesday 10th August

9:19am Had the evening off last night with all the other alternate dayers. They decided to give us an extra day off this session because we missed out on one in the first session – woohoo! A group of us went out to try and find somewhere to stay overnight. Driver John took us, but we couldn't find anywhere that would take counselors, so we ended up just driving around the outskirts of Winkworth for two hours. We went up this really scary road in the dark and were shitting each other up with super scary stories. Pip told me this: A while ago in Australia there were a few cases of the same crime on the long outback roads. Drivers would see something strange in the road so they'd get out to see what it was – it was usually just a doll or a stuffed animal. After realising it was nothing to worry about the driver would get back in his car and carry on. Within a few minutes he'd be sure to look in his rearview mirror and would see someone in the back seat that'd got in when he got out. Then the intruder would rob him, steal his car and sometimes kill him too. That's so, so scary – gives me the chills to think about it again.

We ended up going to MaccyDs, but 'Pat' took so fucking long to serve the ten of us we got a bit rowdy. Management told us they wouldn't serve us again if we came back because we were so disruptive. Haha, barred from McDonalds in Winkworth, that's an achievement as far as I'm concerned. We had to just come back to camp and stay here for the night. Going to Winkworth now though to get brunch and then we're off to Kingfisher Falls for the day.

Thursday 11th August

9:23am We ate at The Copper Kettle for brunch yesterday, which was pretty grim, and then went for a walk around the town. Winkworth basically consists of the drug store Rite Aid, a hunting shop and a few hardware stores. It started to absolutely chuck it down with rain so we went in the hunting shop for cover. We got chatting to the owner after telling him we were from Rockbear.

Him: "I hope you girls don't go walking off camp and around that lake."

Me: "Errm, some of the counselors go running around it and we go there after hours for a break from the kids sometimes."

He stood open-mouthed staring at us.

Him: "Ha, you're not being serious are you?"

He said he would *never* walk around the lake at Rockbear without taking a gun; it's where they purposely go to catch the biggest bears – up to 600 pounders. There was a massive stuffed bear in the shop and he said it was shot at the lake five years ago.

Him: "It's coming up to hunting season so you better put an end to that. There are bears about with cubs. Come between a cub and his mother and that's it for you."

Zoe says she saw a cub the other day although I'm not sure how much I believe her.

He also said Kingfisher Falls was a breeding ground for grass snakes and rattlesnakes and we shouldn't go there either.

Pip: "We go partying down there on days off."

Him: "You girls are insane."

And he walked off.

The rain eased up a bit and we went to Rite Aid to buy a load of shit we don't need. We had nothing better to do with no wheels out of there, so we decided to try to find some fun accommodation again, seeing as Kingfisher Falls was off the agenda with the weather. Everyone else went back to camp for the day, but me, Pip and three of the other girls were determined. We walked to a hotel driver John had told us about, an hour along the highway. Of course the heavy rain started again half an hour after we left so we arrived dripping wet.

Bitch on reception: "Sorry, no camp counselors."

I couldn't believe we were spending our sacred day off walking around in the pissing rain in Winkworth unsuccessfully trying to find a hotel. The only thing for it was to walk back and sit in MaccyDs again. Driver John couldn't pick us up until later as he was dropping off a kid in NYC.

Luckily Pat wasn't on shift so we sat in there for two hours just messing about and scoffing chicken nuggets while watching the rain bounce off the pavements. A bunch of guys came in and randomly Pip knew one of them from back home. They were working at another camp up the road. They told us about this house, which belongs to an old woman who rents it out to counselors – they'd stayed there a few nights ago. Pip's friend made a few calls and sorted it for us to stay that night. What a guy!

We went and brought shit loads of alcohol and then made our way over the road to the address. The house was wall-to-wall chintz with tea sets on every surface, pictures of old women in strange hats on the walls and carpets with enough pattern to make your eyes bleed. It definitely looked like an old lady's house. I bet she's got cats somewhere too. There were four rooms and the beds looked amazing – I hadn't seen a duvet for over two months. It was only $30 each; all we had to do was leave the money by the door. She's a very trusting old dear. It was already 7pm by the time we got there and I couldn't wait to get in bed. We sat around the table scoffing the munchies with the TV on in the background. It felt like we were just in one of our student houses, it was great. We started playing drinking games and quickly got absolutely wasted. Pip and me had this lethal vodka that was the cheapest in the shop. We were conked out on the sofa by about 9:30pm.

I woke up at 4am and watched the news with one of the many beers we hadn't had time to drink. I felt like a real Winkworth hick kicking back with a can. An hour or so later I heard noises upstairs; Pip was bent double retching over the delicately decorated bathroom tub. Big lumps of bright orange Cheetos crisps were spewed down the side and I'm sure I spied a bit of stomach lining in there too. We had about half an hour before our taxi was due to arrive to get us back to camp so using my fingers, I squashed the lumps down the plug hole while simultaneously rubbing her back to try and help her get it all up. She was a state. I woke the other three girls up and we managed to get the house relatively in order in time for our taxi. I felt so bad for abusing the dainty cottage, we left a good tip and a loving message in the visitors' book to try and make up for it. I hope the lingering cheesy sick smell won't put her off renting it out to other counselors in the future. Maybe all the other hotels had the right idea.

We left at seven to make it back in time to get the kids up for breakfast. I'm gutted we wasted the opportunity for a lush comfy bed with proper sheets. Poor Pip: all the colour had drained from her face. She looked traumatised. We stashed the leftover beer in the bushes on the way to the GC to drink later, as long as the taxi driver doesn't tell Earl that is – you don't know who's watching you here.

Pip was so ill all day. Visual arts is definitely the best department to be in when you're hungover – we're in the shade and the air drifts through. At lunch I saw one of the other girls who was with us. She teaches dance in the sweaty studios – and looked like death. Apparently a few of the guys, including Ben, had come looking for us to stay over, but couldn't find the house. Unlucky, although I guess it could've been fun!

2:03pm Just got my iPod – it's literally incredible.

9:03pm Zoe's getting ready to go to the GC. Damn, she looks well cool. I don't know why she bothers going; she doesn't drink because she's going to be famous and doesn't want dodgy photos of her getting out, and she's not into guys and never has been in case they do a kiss and tell on her. Boring!

Cara and me tried to get out on the bikes again today, but the Polish dude wouldn't let us. She's gone right off him now – she can't have a 'dry shite' for a boyfriend. We just sat eating sweets from the vending machines instead. Also, we've booked our Mexico holiday, woohoo! We just decided to go all out and empty our bank accounts. A week in Cancun in an apartment with two double beds – cannot wait!

I made a well cool rocket today, now all the kids want one. All the materials are running out so I stuck loads of leftover scraps to the main base with the hot glue gun and a stick of dynamite on the side, and it looks wicked. My creativity is wasted in this place.

1am I've felt really homesick today, probably because all my campers are and I'm hungover. Now I can't get to sleep. Four weeks today I'll be home, I'm ready for it and will be happy when the time comes, but I'll also be really sad too. I'm going back to the hard work of third year and debt too, eugh. It's not like I'm always thinking about home or wanting to be there, it's only when something bad happens here, or someone gets a *heat* magazine or some Cadbury's chocolate that I give it a moment's thought. It's actually surprised me how little I have thought about home.

My relationship with Rebecca is also upsetting me a lot too. We loved each other at the start and it's such a shame she turned out to be so fucking annoying. We could've been great friends. When I first met her I thought she was amazing, but something changed in her. I don't know if it was something I did or what, but she's gone really introverted and just doesn't speak to me anymore. Maybe we were just too similar, and had our fill of each other at the start. It's so hard living and working so intensely with someone you've never met before for three months. She says she's got this tinnitus thing – which is like a ringing in the ears – I guess that must be pissing her off too, as it means she can't play violin in the pit at the performances. No need to take it out on me though.

I wish I was in my nice, clean bed at home right now, ooo with fresh sheets, that would be amazing.

I was really needy towards Ben today; his timetable and mine are so incompatible this session, it's rubbish. I never see him. I thought I had him to myself in rest hour, but then people always come over so we had to talk to them. I can never talk to him on my own – argh! He's mine. Well kind of, apart from the bitch girlfriend. I was talking to Cara about him today. I don't know how I'll feel when we leave. It's going to be strange and sad to go, but then I don't think he's the love of my life or anything. I just really like being with him and we've had such a good summer together. We've started to get really close again – I need to keep the fact that he has a girlfriend and lives on the other side of the world in my mind to stop myself getting carried away.

Another reason I'm so homesick is that so much is happening at home; I just feel I should be there. Mum's definitely having the operation on her kidney, which is really scary. Also, my best friend from when I was like five is trying to cope with her parents' divorce and my brother and his girlfriend have split up. I guess I couldn't really do anything in any of these situations, but I just feel so distant with this happening to my most favourite people in the world. I know if I was home I'd be bored out of my brain. It's going to be so weird to go back. I don't know how I'll just slot back into normal life when I've had such an incredible summer.

Friday 12th August

9:13am Meal times have got really weird between me, Zoe and Rebecca. I remember at the start of camp when Rebecca and me always wanted to sit together and we'd be annoyed when the head counselor asked us to scatter among the campers. Now I go one end, Rebecca goes the other and Zoe sits in the middle, and we don't say a word to each other. The kids must be able to pick up on it. Zoe's always up and down talking to the other counselors and Rebecca just stares off into space. I'm so sure there's nothing actually wrong with her though – she's just over-dramatic and loves people thinking there's something wrong with her when there's not.

One of my campers has quit her show because she couldn't cope with being a lead here while her mum is at home fighting cancer. She said that she'd come here for some fun and not to have more stresses. I can absolutely, definitely see her point, but they're five days out of 12 into rehearsals and she was the lead so she's kind of left them in the lurch. These kids have got their heads screwed on though, they seem much more mature and in touch with their feelings and each other than I was at that age. I'm convinced that my drinking from such a young age has stunted me emotionally. Me and my mates just used to get pissed together – these girls actually sit and talk about their feelings.

One of my campers, Tegan, did something really weird today. She was wearing her stepbrother's hat and then took it off, sniffed it hard and was like, "mmmmm", in some sexily appreciative way with her eyes fluttering.

Tegan: "Uhh, I just love the way he smells."

She took another long lungful. I was speechless, I'm sure that's not a normal thing to do.

8:32pm I felt like getting up to some mischief in rest hour today. I went off to see what Cara was up to – she's always good for a laugh. We ended up in a three-legged race against ourselves along the main pathway of camp with our legs tied together with plastic bags. Of course, just as we were turning the corner we bumped into Bud. He was not impressed, although, he didn't actually tell us off. I'm sure he found it funny really. Cara's so sweet when she thinks she's going to get in trouble, she goes all quiet and earnest, like butter wouldn't melt. She puts on this wide-eyed innocent face and just looks to me for answers, wilting under authority. She got off scot-free and he sent her back to her bunk as she has the youngest kids to look after and is meant to be with them at all times. I was made to go up to the front office and monitor how long the kids spent on the phones to their parents. Usually I enjoy listening in on other people's conversations, but some of these kids are sad, sad, sad.

I was reminded that although I see camp as some super cool place I'd have given anything to come for, some of the kids are sent here because their super-rich parents just want rid of them for the summer. I heard them pleading to go home, but their parents won't let them. They're probably too busy sunning themselves in the South of France or some equally exotic location.

When I got back to the bunk I wished I was still up there – Rebecca and her mate were still banging on about their 'boyfriends', who aren't actually their boyfriends.

Me (in my head): 'THEY ARE NOTHING SPECIAL!'

They were squashed into the corner of the bunk gossiping while the kids were running wild around them. I'm pretty sure the boys they're discussing won't be holed up in a corner talking about them. They'll be spending their time more wisely, off priming other girls most likely.

11:17pm I'm amazed at how much I'm learning being here. I know I laugh at the kids for only knowing one place in England – London – but when I talk to the other counselors from other countries I'm just as thick. There are a few white girls from South Africa, which really confused me at first. How could I not know white people lived in South Africa? Really, how can I not know that? I thought South Africa was all starving children in mud huts.

Also, talking to the Australians, I never knew that the lived-in part of Australia was all along the coast and that it took so long to get across country. Pip and Zoe live about three hours apart but Pip was like, "ah, it's just round the corner". They have no water system in the centre so no one lives there and that's where the outback is that you hear so much about on the soaps – I never knew that. Pip finds it hilarious that the Brits are all so into *Neighbours* and *Home and Away*, they don't even watch it over there.

Saturday 13th August

7:17pm My old camper Keakuki has made me so sad today, and whenever I've seen her over the past few weeks actually. She's 13, it's been almost nine weeks, and her parents have never visited her once. They haven't even sent a letter, or any treats in the post. She keeps begging the head counselor to go home, but her parents obviously don't want her there, so there's nothing we can do. Keakuki must know this – that's obviously why she's such hard work – she's going to have some big, big issues as she grows up. I can't imagine spending so long without talking to my parents, especially at that age. It will be *three* months by the time she sees them. She must be from some super-rich family to afford 12 weeks at summer camp – the bill would be around $14,000. She's the only kid I know here for the four sessions; she's not going to have a summer at home with her friends and family.

My camper Tegan – the hat sniffer – and another one who will probably need a psychologist to explain her 'relationship' with her stepbrother, is driving me crazy. She's always in the bunk when I'm on my break and tells me it's because she's sick. She lies there all day and won't eat, and I have to spend my break trying to get her out of the bunk or counseling her to see what's wrong. Then when I see her in the evenings up at the canteen she's laughing and dancing away while stuffing her face with pizza and ice cream. I asked her about it last night, but then felt really mean because she was having fun and it made her pretend to be all sick and down. It pisses me off so much to see her there on my break though when there's nothing wrong with her, that precious hour is my time.

9:51pm Rebecca, Zoe and me had a chat this evening – not about anything in particular – but it definitely cleared the air between us a bit. Our main problem is that we just stopped talking. When I look back I think it started with us all getting a bit annoyed with each other and I'm guessing that individually we decided to cope with this by only talking when we had to. This has led to none of us actually communicating with each other at all. At camp your relationship with your co-counselors is fragile, but vital to your bunk's happiness. It's like a marriage, you need to constantly communicate to look after the kids properly and to support each other. I need to take some tips from everything I've been noting about how the campers relate to each other, and if something upsets me, just say so then it's out in the open and it can be dealt with. I never actually found out what's been wrong with Rebecca all this time, but at least we spoke.

Zoe really fancies Caleb from rock shop, even though he's with this beautiful American counselor from Pip's bunk. As a couple they're probably the coolest and best-looking people on camp, but Zoe has decided that he's the one for her. In her quest to get him she wrote Caleb a letter without signing it, telling him that his girlfriend was slutting it about with all the guys at camp and that she thought he should know. What the fuck? How immature is that? The worst thing is, Caleb knows it was Zoe. She's been stalking him for days and the American counselor heard it was her from one of her campers, as Zoe stupidly put the note on her bed herself. She has just made an *absolute* twat of herself.

Since finding this out, for some reason Rebecca has decided she wants to be best friends with Caleb's girlfriend. She's such a rocker wannabe. She's getting Caleb to put dreads in her hair like his. I'm sure she thinks it will go with this whole angsty vibe she's creating. It's like she doesn't think being happy suits her anymore. When she does smile or say anything in a jolly way it seems fake.

1:13am Tonight Pip and me ran through the bunks screaming when the kids were asleep, just for a minute. It seemed funny at the time – after drinking up at the GC – but definitely won't be if one of the kids dobs on us, and it doesn't actually seem that funny now either. We could get in so much trouble. Why are we such twats? I just feel like being naughty at the moment because it's nearly the end. It's like the end of school when you feel all giddy and silly because you're allowed to go in non-uniform.

Sunday 14th August

10:30am Every single time I see her...
Asperger's girl: "You're horrible."
I don't respond so she starts shouting at the top of her voice.

Asperger's girl: "Lucy's horrible, Lucy's horrible."
I ignore her, but then she's like, "I was joking," and starts begging me to be her friend, causing even more of a fuss. It's so embarrassing – I feel like a mum with a child having a tantrum. I really can't be bothered to talk to her anymore.

12:17pm There was a massive storm today – it was so cool. I was sunbathing down at waterfront on my break and then within five minutes raindrops literally the size of golf balls were bouncing off the ground. We had to run with all these screaming little kids to the gym. They were so scared of the thunder and lightning. The water iceberg flew over to rock shop – they had to catch it and tie it down – and the waterfront pier moved out of place. We heard a tree snap and the crash as it fell down – it was so scary and went on for about an hour. The little kids were so cute shivering in their swimsuits and sucking their thumbs. It's amazing how it makes you feel inside when a little kid wants to snuggle up to you, even if they are just using you for warmth.

12:58pm I feel like Ben and me have just slotted back into our old roles together again. We're all lovey dovey and I'm actually really enjoying it. The other night at the GC one of the lifeguards kept buying me drinks and was trying to chat me up, but I just wanted to be with Ben. I wish we *could* be together in the real world. I love him, no I don't, I didn't just write that.

7:19pm Pip and me were called to go up to the camp director's office earlier. We were absolutely shitting ourselves that one of the kids had told on us for running through the bunks. I was convinced we were going to be fired at the final hurdle. When we got there the receptionist didn't know what we were talking about though. Zoe was tricking us, bitch. Hmmm, need to think of something good now to menace her back.

Rebecca's little camp boyfriend split up with her today, can't remember why. Boring. Hopefully she'll stop banging on about him. Caleb, the guy from rock shop, has finished her dreads – they look shit. Apparently while he was doing them he asked Rebecca why Zoe sent that letter.
Rebecca: "It was so embarrassing that he thought *I'd* know. As if I'm friends with her or something..."

It was actually a really stupid, cringey thing of Zoe to do. Weirdo. And how very *dare* she put Princess Rebecca in a situation like that?

1am There are just two weeks left at camp, very sad, but I'm looking forward to no more shitty kids/visual arts/rules. Although, I did have a panic earlier that in two weeks I won't see any of these people all day, every day again. I'm used to them now, and the thought of having time alone seems crazy. I remember jewellery Jo saying in the first few weeks, something like, "Yeah of course I'm back at camp. When else do you have all your best friends on your doorstep?" I now realise how true that is.

In particular, of course, I'm thinking about Ben. Is it weird that we haven't even thought about travelling together after camp? I guess so. He's travelling America with another guy and I'm going to Mexico. End of. I think when the whole girlfriend thing happened it jolted me back to reality. We're not meant to be together and nothing long-lasting would ever happen, because we live thousands of miles apart. I need to stop liking him so much, I guess we're both just enjoying it for what it is now and that's why it's so good at the moment. I hope this isn't the most I'm ever going to get on with a guy though, it can't be.

Monday 15th August

5:45pm My campers are kind of annoying me now, I've had enough. They're all so down and depressed and it's having a domino effect on all of them, and on me. I think it stems from Tegan lying in bed all the time, the girl whose mum has cancer spending all day crying in the bunk and Rebecca's current attitude. I really don't know what I can do to help them. It doesn't make for a great atmosphere for the other campers. My other camper, Helen, seems to keep rubbing people up the wrong way too. There's always someone looking for her on camp and I'm pretty sure it's not for positive reasons. I just want to tell them to chill out and have fun, which is what Zoe did yesterday. Rebecca was well pissed off with her though – she wants them to follow their feelings to encourage them to blossom or some hippy shit like that. I think they need a kick up the arse to make them join in all the opportunities around them instead of moping around in the bunk.

Zoe was even *more* useless earlier than usual; I'm amazed it's possible, to be honest. The camper with the gluten allergy collapsed and then started screaming in some sort of fit and Zoe couldn't even be arsed to get out of bed to help. I had to send one of the other kids to find the head counselor. She's such a bad counselor she's actually a danger to the children.

I did get to see the medical room though. There are a ridiculous amount of cough drops in there lined up in jars – I took a good handful just for snacks. The nurse had a huge glass-fronted lockable drugs store that was filled to the brim with packets of pills. I don't know how she manages to keep track of them all. There were two beds down either wall and the nurse's desk was at the front. I weighed myself while I was there, pheweee, definitely too many chicken wings this summer!

I'm missing the evening activity tonight because I have to stay in the bunk with gluten-allergy girl. The girls compete against the boys in everything: singing, dancing, acting, playing instruments, running, swimming, even in lining up to get into dinner. They've been talking about it all week and they've got the day off majors and minors to practice. I can hear them singing some song they've made up to the tune of *Hollaback Girl* by Gwen Stefani. Although, can't say I'm that bothered to be missing it. All I have to do is stay in the bunk so she has someone here so it's a bit of a rest for me. She's making weird deep breathing noises like she can't catch enough breath. Hope she doesn't die on me. She's so small and skinny and fragile, she needs some meat on her bones.

8:12pm Got some of my pay today – $400. I think that's a third, so I'll be getting $1200, which sounds right. That will be $200 for up to August 29th, $600 for Mexico and $400 for when Cara and me go to NYC for a few days after Mexico. Woohoo!

12:34am Oh god, *the* most stressful night ever with my campers. All seven of them had some sort of issue and Rebecca and Zoe were both out on their night off.
– Tegan was crying hysterically about her stepbrother being sent to hospital after hitting his head. She was convinced he'd die.
– Another one was bent over double with some sort of stomach cramps, she couldn't even walk up to the infirmary.

– Helen has been thrown out of the play she was in for bullying the other kids, so she was bitching about that and making sure everyone else paid for it.
– The girl whose mum has cancer was sure her mum had died in the night and the front office wouldn't phone her to check. I had to get the head counselor to force them to let her use the phone. She was fine, of course.
– Gluten-allergy girl collapsed again when she stood up from lying down after an anxiety attack.
– Another one is spending the night in the medical room because of a temperature, and who's the last one?
– Oh, the super. She was off out having pizza with the other supers.

The head counselor was frantically running in and out trying calm them all down, while I was having visions of apologising to the kids' parents over the phone about their child's demise. It was not fun.

Tuesday 16th August

12:16pm There's a definite uniform evolving at Camp Rockbear. Over the last few weeks you see more and more counselors with the little white iPod buds in their ears – a combination of some generous tips and of being well and truly sick of the kids and doing anything for a few moments of peace I think. I'm using mine at meal times to block them out – it's bad, but looking around the canteen all the other counselors are at it too. Most counselors, and campers, have brightly coloured water bottles, colourful beads, silk-screened t-shirts, denim shorts and Birkenstocks. There's usually something Abercrombie and Fitch thrown in there too. Oh and all the counselors have the keys to their departments around their necks too, on a piece of lanyard from visual arts.

Cara and me went down to the climbing wall on our break today and tried to do the Leap of Faith. It's a 30-foot tower you have to climb using the grips and when you get to the top you jump off and try and grab this rubber chicken. I was shitting it all the way up. I couldn't stand up my legs were shaking so much. One of the climbing counselors could see I was struggling and came up behind me to coax me to the top.
Fit climbing counselor: "Come on Lucy, you can do it."
Little kids waiting to climb: "Hurry up Lucy, just climb. It's easy!"

Fit climbing counselor: "Put your left foot on that yellow grip there."
Me (screeching): "Which one is left?!"

I could barely look down to see the coloured grip, never mind bring my fucking foot up to reach it. It was mortifying. I was in the most unattractive position possible with that harness strapped around my arse, and to make it worse the fit Swedish counselor came around the corner filming his video postcard. I'm sure my bum making its way up a 12-foot pylon is not how he wants to remember camp, but he carried on filming and gave me a little wave with his eye glued to the viewfinder, bastard. I could hear Cara at the bottom of the pole absolutely pissing herself laughing. The embarrassment of the situation gave me the oomph I needed to get up to the top. I didn't look down and just jumped off, making a half-hearted attempt to reach for the chicken – absolutely, definitely not doing that again.

8:16pm More evidence to the fact Cara and me aren't liked up at visual arts: we're the only ones not asked to help with the annual plaque. It's this carved wood thing that goes in the dining hall to commemorate each year. They're having these secret meetings to make it, but it's only Cara and me who aren't in on the secret. Visual arts is the only department not having an end of summer party, although because of this I'm a bit skeptical that it's just that me and Cara aren't invited.

One of the second-session bitches dobbed me in for skiving off the tie-dye class I'm meant to be teaching with her. I absolutely don't blame her, but I really can't be bothered to go, that's my time with Ben and I love having two frees a day. I've only done it the last week. I know it's naughty, but we only ever have three or four kids a lesson I don't see why we both have to be there. I'd be prepared to negotiate and compromise – I wouldn't mind if we took it in turns to skive, but she wasn't into the idea.

Inspired by my creation the other day Cara and me have invented a new spin on rocketry, 'Creative Rockets'. It basically means we use all the scrap we can find in the rocketry room and hot glue them onto a tube before adding a stick of dynamite. They look shit and I'm a bit worried about the safety aspect, but the kids love them and that's the main thing.

Wednesday 17th August

8:46am Had another staff meeting last night. The head counselor kept us behind afterwards to talk about the bunk: she said our camper Helen had ripped some pages out of one of my other campers' bible – what the fuck? She keeps being racist to her and using the N-word when she talks to her, thinking she's cool and funny. There are barely any black kids at camp; I've never thought about that, but it must be really hard for her if she's being singled out like this by horrible Helen. Helen is purposely leaving her out as much as possible and generally being as mean as she can. The head counselor said that she'd already spoken to her while we were at the meeting and told her she can't go around saying that. If she does she will be in big trouble and chucked off camp, so we need to keep an eye out for it happening again. I don't understand how none of us noticed this was going on – the poor girl. Considering we've only got seven girls this session, they're bloody hard work.

After the meeting Danielle, Ben, Danielle's current guy Mickey and me, went to watch a DVD in the video room. We had the spare mattresses out and we were well cosy watching it on the projector screen with some coco pops from the dining hall as munchies. The visual arts boss came in and she did not look happy. She's really pissing me off at the moment – she's so rude to me and I haven't done anything to her. People are always watching stuff in here, bet she doesn't look at them like shit.

The film finished at about two and I thought Ben and me were just going to have a nice sexy walk back to the bunks, but then Mickey put on some comedy shit. I hate American stand-up. I really hate it when comedians keep repeating themselves because they think it's funnier. I stayed though, hoping Ben and me would get a chance to be alone together at the end. Then at about three, Ben's like, "I'm going to bed". I couldn't believe I'd sat through an hour of that shit in the hope of some love at the end and then he was just going to leave by himself. I just got up and walked off. I was so annoyed as I walked across the basketball courts back to my bunk, fuming in fact. Then I saw someone dart across the main path really fast. I got back to my bunk and Ben was there, totally out of breath. Yay! He picked me up and kissed me like they do in the movies – it was so cheesy, but I loved it. He said he wouldn't have been able to sleep if he'd thought I was annoyed. Ah so cute. Then we went and 'slept' in the staff room instead. Toot toot!

12:12pm In sunshine time I went down to the lower arts block to pay a little visit to the snack machines. One of the rocketry boys was there with a rod he'd made out of some old wire and the glue block from a Prittstick. He was fishing out all the dropped coins from under the slats on the cabin floor. He proudly showed me his pocket full of nickels and had a huge grin on his face.
Him: "I'm rich!"

I'm really going to miss my daily walk along the path from my bunk to the visual arts department. I probably end up doing it about three times a day, at a good 10 minutes a time. I love the fresh, dewy morning when I'm on my way to work and then by lunch when I have to walk back it's hot, hot, hot. I'll never be able to recreate that delicious fresh smell of the woodland air – you don't get that in Sheffield City Centre.

Gluten-girl's mum came to pick her up. She didn't even find me to say bye *and* her mum didn't even say thanks, or leave a tip. Charming.

6:30pm Went to help teach tie-dye today – boring. The bitch who dobbed me in didn't let me do anything and made me feel like one of her kids. Fuck that. I really don't know how everyone else exists on just one free a day. I love having two where for one I can chill out and the other hang out with Ben or Cara.

Saw Jamie's girlfriend earlier, she's with some other guy from video now. It's weird she's moved on so quick, but then, I guess she did only actually know Jamie for about two weeks. I'm sure his death will affect her forever, but it's not like she has all these lasting memories of him. They didn't have time to make any.

9:39pm Tonight's evening activity was a 'dance' on the basketball courts. Basically just a normal canteen night, but all the kids were a bit more dressed up and the night is made into more of an occasion. I was with Pip, Emily and a few other girls on area duty to bust kids getting sexy around the gym and circus when Ben came along with his tarot cards. We lay on the big gym mats while he read each of our cards. My first card, my past card, was the hermit – Ben said that this meant in some areas of my life I'm extrovert and in others I'm really introverted. He said that I was a very private and closed person who didn't like to rely on anyone else and was very independent. He said I was very much my own person and that meant a lot to me. It's weird: he's so right, and it's not stuff I have ever said to him, ever. My present card was, I can't remember, but I do remember he said it meant I was learning a lot about myself. I was becoming more accepting of people and more open. I was beginning to trust others and realise that I needed them. The future card was someone sitting down at a desk. Ben said this meant in the future I will be a hard worker and will work hard for myself. He said I was good at what I do and I need to prepare to work hard for what I want in life. He knows so much stuff about me. Although, I'm still undecided as to whether it really is a talent or if he's just good at interpreting people.

He said stuff to Pip that she said psychics had told her before. They always talk about her having children and being surrounded by them. We ended up sitting there for two hours chatting about freaky shit that's happened to us – not paying any attention to the kids who were probably frolicking all around us. Emily says she has out-of-body experiences where she'll wake up in the morning in her mind and she'll feel herself move and get out of bed, but her body is actually still lying there. Freaky!

Thursday 18th August

6:08am I'm disgustingly hungover and off to Niagara Falls, woo! A few of us went round the lake last night to get drunk on the bottle of Jack Daniels I'd had in my bag for too long. I'd forgotten about it. Wow, there's been so many reasons for Earl to fire me this summer and I've managed to get away with all of them, so far anyway.

We just ended up chatting shit – mostly about sex, as usual – all night. Danielle has slept with 38 people, fuck! And Ben with 26, I couldn't believe it. That seems loads, but I guess they're both older than me. I don't really care about Ben's number though, as long as it's not over 50 or less than two.

I stupidly chose that moment to relay what the hunting shop owner man told me about the bears. Danielle was really pissed off with me that I hadn't said anything before. All the other people who were in the shop at the time could've said too, but of course it was me who got the blame. She upset me actually. She can be such a bitch to me sometimes considering how nice I am too her. It's weird, she just flips and gets really mardy and totally contradicts herself. I think the honeymoon is over with us two. It's nearly the end of camp and people are definitely showing their true colours. I'm so glad I'm not going on holiday with her, she's going to Florida with Pete – I can guarantee those two will fight like cat and dog.

It got to about three and just me, Pip and Ben were left. It was freezing so we decided to head back. Ben and me were just laughing at Pip who was stumbling across the road and babbling about the cold night. We dropped Pip off at her bunk and then walked down to waterfront and ended up getting a bit rampant on the picnic bench. Came back at 4:30amish as the sun was coming up to try and avoid getting busted.

So I had about an hour's sleep and then Pip woke me up to go to Niagara Falls!

10am Just slept away the four-hour journey, brilliant. Got well cosy with the blanket Britney left me, I knew she was useful for something. Nearly there, hello Canada – I can see you!

11:23pm Niagara Falls was incredible. We stayed on the America side and went on the Maid in the Mist boat trip; we were in the middle of Horseshoe Falls with the water falling all around us. We walked around the caves and up to the hurricane deck. Emily and me just stood there screaming "Ni-a-ga-ra" at the top of our voices while the water blasted at us. We went on the trolley tram around the top of the Falls and it was incredible to look down at it all – the Maid in the Mist seemed tiny from up there. The gushing water was so loud – I kept needing a wee.

Danielle, Emily, a few others and me went through the border controls to the Canada side just to get the stamp in our passports. The legal drinking age is 18 there so we officially drank for the first time since we left our home countries. I'd actually forgotten the legal age was 21 in America; no one has asked me for ID here, ever. We had dinner at Planet Hollywood. I had a delicious Jolly Rancher cocktail and a few shots – looted the cool branded glasses obviously. They were £10 in the shop downstairs. I had grilled salmon marinated in maple syrup as an ode to Canada and it was delicious. Emily went to the bank and realised she'd spent all her money – so I bought her dinner until we get paid. It's mad how much you spend at camp. You think you're coming for a free ride but with all the booze and trips to Walmart it just disappears.

After dinner we went to Hershey's Chocolate Factory and had strawberries dipped in chocolate for pudding. We had to be quick though – it's a four-hour journey back to camp. An incredible last day off!

Friday 19th August

12:17pm The kids couldn't be bothered to clean up today so instead of nagging them, I just did it. Tegan felt so bad she helped me; I should've taken this approach before. I just want to chill out and have fun for these last few days, not spend all my time shouting at the kids. They have been pretty good about it compared to the last girls though. I'm definitely getting more patient with the kids now. Actually, it's probably a mixture of more patience and me not caring so much what they think anymore.

Skived off tie-dye again today, so boring! I've just realised that I've been teaching painting and drawing for two weeks and in that time I haven't drawn or painted a single thing. I'm shit. I just hand out the paper and pens and leave them to it. Halfway through I'll go around and make some supportive comments and a few oohs and aahs and that's it, job done.

9:49pm The kitchen staff put on a second 'banquet' for everyone today. It was really tasty, obviously would have been better with a glass of wine though. The hors d'oeuvres were so nice: shrimp and prawns and duck. Everyone had made the effort – curled hair, best clothes and even a bit of make-up – this must be what everyone looks like at home, away from the scrub of camp.
Ben: "You look absolutely stunning."

He looked like he was going to cry. Bless him. God I really fancy him. He had a little bow tie on and looked lush. Wish he was English and didn't already have a girlfriend he wanted to make babies with; we could have some beautiful little sprogs ourselves.

They presented the plaque made by all of visual arts – except for Cara and me of course – to Earl. It was shit. We could have done better with a few mop heads and googley eyes for sure.

The performing arts staff did a 30-minute version of *Grease* for evening activity. Zoe was absolutely brilliant as Rizzo and Earl played the guardian angel – all the kids were screaming with laughter, and a few of the counselors too.

I really wanted to go out afterwards as everyone was in such good spirits, but I was on duty. I begged the head counselor to let the super counselor be on duty by herself, but she wasn't having it. If I couldn't go to the party, then the party could come to us. I was winding the kids up and generally being very hyper playing loud music and having pillow fights with the girls next door. My campers started talking about sex and then the 17-year-old super told them all she'd first done it when she was 12; I definitely didn't appreciate her telling the 13-year-old girls that, especially Tegan – she worships the ground the super walks on. Not much I could do about it after she'd said it, but they just seem so young, innocent and impressionable and I don't want them corrupted by her slutty ways.

The girls were dancing on the bunk rafters, it was pretty funny yet highly dangerous. I'd get bollocked if the head counselor saw me letting them do that. Awww, they were telling me they thought Ben was really cute, and that we made a really sweet couple. Then Pip burst in...

Pip: "Lucy, help, I don't know what to do."

I followed her through the bathroom to her bunk and the girl who everyone ribs for being a lesbian was sat on her bunk crying and trying to slice her wrists with a pair of scissors. She'd managed to draw some blood, but definitely nothing life threatening. I took them off her and gave her a hug. I don't know how serious it was, like whether she was doing it for attention or what. The girls are just unbelievably nasty to each other sometimes – especially her and Helen; I think those two have some long-standing rivalry. I'm not surprised they feel so down. This was surely a cry for help though. If you really wanted to hurt yourself you wouldn't do it using a pair of scissors with counselors around and surrounded by campers. The head counselor came and took her up to the front office.

Saturday 20th August

10:32am I'm starting to think a lot of kids just come to rocketry to laugh at Cara and me. The numbers are increasing every day. It's generally younger kids, but there's this 16-year-old super nerdy girl who comes religiously too. She doesn't ever speak, but I guess she must be having a good time in the class to keep coming back. She creeps me out.

7:22pm Zoe got a bollocking from Bud and the head counselor for being shit today. It's a bit pointless now and they could have done it a while ago, but at least she got one; she's useless. She was well pissed off – think she's blaming it on Rebecca though, her and the head counselor are like best friends. Rebecca told me once that the reason she's never won the Counselor of the Week award is because her and our head counselor are too good friends and people would say it was favouritism if she ever won. Ha, that little one made me laugh. As if!

Rebecca's favourite boy, and so top topic of conversation this week, is one of the guys from rock shop. She keeps going on about how they're going to travel Texas together and all this bullshit. Last night he came up to me when I was drunk in the staff room and was blatantly chatting me up, and trying to feel me up too. He's a fitty, but obviously Rebecca likes him – so I'd never go there – and I'm with Ben of course. She's deluding herself if she thinks there's something between them, she's got man attachment issues that girl.

I genuinely think Rebecca and her little friend from the kitchen hate the fact that Ben and me have made it through the whole summer. I know it's only been eight weeks since he arrived in the second lot of counselors, but an eight-week relationship at camp is a long time. Every day is like a week here, so much happens and there's so much to keep up with. She was mocking me a bit today, but you know that kind of mocking girls do when they're actually jealous? Yeah, it was kind of like that.

9:19pm Evening activity tonight was an orchestra concert. I had my iPod in with my hair down to block it all out and looked up just in time to see Earl storming over to us. I was absolutely bricking it. He looked irate and his eyes were pussing – a sure sign he's after blood. Thankfully he just bollocked the boys behind me for talking, and then cancelled the Rocky Horror Midnight Parade, which seems a bit harsh. Every year the kids dress up in their best fishnets and leather corsets to walk around the camp at the strike of 12 singing songs from the show. The kids have been talking about it since they arrived. That is not going to be a popular decision.

1:21am Just been to the GC. I haven't been there for so long, but it was a really good night. Gay Pete and me were getting really down and depressed at the thought of leaving though – we've only got eight days to go so we're on the final countdown now. Danielle was saying how good Ben and me are together and that it's amazing how well we get on. It was nice to hear. Hmmm, getting a bit jealous of him and Rebecca's mate though. I know she's really flirty with everyone, but she's said before that she thinks Ben's really interesting and good-looking and Ben has said he thinks she's really sexy before too. Hands off bitch.

The highlight of the night was a well funny photo of Cara and Emily with their trousers around their ankles doing a wee on the main road separating the GC and the camp – you could see the stream going downhill. We're feral – how will we cope when we rejoin the real world?

We got back to camp and Pete was making out he was cold.
Pete: "Could I just borrow your Levi's jacket, just to walk back to my bunk?"
His bunk is about a three-minute walk away and he's been admiring that jacket since the first week. I let him, but if I ever see that jacket again I'll be amazed. He's such a pikey, but he gets away with it because he's such a charmer, and fit.

Sunday 21st August
6:16pm Lazy day, woohoo! Pip and me lay in bed for two hours just talking about home and our families. She told me her mum has cancer. Pip had wanted to come to camp forever, but because the Australian school year runs from January to December they have to take a whole year off to come here. This was the first and only year she could do it really because of school and university, so her mum pretty much made her come. Pip's so positive and fun – you'd never know she had anything so awful going on. She started to get a bit emotional thinking about her mum. I didn't really know what to say. Her family sound so funny – I can't wait to go and stay with them next year when I go to Australia. She said that when she gets back home she's going to train to be a teacher – she'll be amazing at that. I love her even more now.

They announced on the loudspeakers it was time for everyone to come up to the car park to go to the cinema. Pip and me were still in our pyjamas in her bed. My kids ran in to get us up. Haha, we're so shit when we get together. After a quick change we blamed the kids for us being late and we left to see *Willy Wonka* at Winkworth Cinema. On the bus on the way there Pip and me had all the kids singing random songs. We got through the whole of *Bohemian Rhapsody* in one attempt and by the time we were finished we were practically there.

10:21pm When we got back it was my turn to DJ up at canteen. Keakuki went absolutely mental at me and was hysterical because she wanted to help, but I said no because there were already about 10 kids queuing up to be allowed into the DJ booth to put their songs on. She was just screaming my name and looked like she was going to cry. It's scary how frustrated she gets when she doesn't get her own way. I've noticed her getting worse and worse over the summer. She seems to have forgotten about the great relationship we had at the start, probably because I let her get away with too much so she thinks she can be like this with me. I know she misses her parents, but she's taking it out on the wrong person.

Haha, I can see Cara coming towards me and wow, she's changed out of her pyjama bottoms for once. It's actually weird to see her in normal clothes – well, when I say normal: pink skirt, pink top, pink flip-flops and even pink earphones. She's happily singing away to her music oblivious to the world. She's always listening to 90s pop like Britney, or anything by the Vengaboys; no wonder she's so happy all the time, yet slightly crazy too.

12:16am Cara went to Niagara Falls today with all the other normal-day-off counselors. She, Ben, Pete, this guy Bailey, and a few others all went and got drunk at Planet Hollywood. Her and Bailey – who's a right fitty – got on really well and so she sat next to him on the bus on the way back to camp.

Cara: "We were just talking and laughing together... and then... errrmm..."

She wouldn't finish the sentence. She just kept laughing and looking away – she was killing me.

Cara: "... in the end... errr... I gave him a blow job under the blanket."

I actually couldn't stop laughing.

Cara: "Then we stopped at Walmart and when everyone went to get

on the bus afterwards, I swear to god, the boys were fighting over who was going to sit next to me."
Too, too funny. Filth bag.

Monday 22nd August

12:07pm Last night there were two car crashes. The janitor's friend overturned his car after driving it back drunk from Winkworth and two of the counselors found it and were apparently hysterical, as you would be. They said the friend found it really funny as he got out the wreckage, and seemed really pissed – what an absolute fucking dickhead. I can't believe someone would do that after everything that's happened this summer and all the upset and pain it's caused. I never would have before, but after this summer I will never, ever, ever, drive drunk, ever.

The other one was this counselor from costume who got in a car with a local hick she'd met at the GC, pretty stupid anyway. He dropped her back at camp and then drove off and crashed into a tree. No one was hurt, but they're so stupid, annoying and selfish – Earl will go mental and probably never let anyone leave camp ever again if he finds out.

8:16pm I've been thinking a lot about my life at home today, and how coming to camp has changed it. I lost three stone to do camp because I didn't want to be the fat one – I'm still so proud of myself for managing to do it. If I'd gone on living as I was, and as everyone around me was, I would never have known what I was capable of. My relationship with Ben has given me so much more confidence with guys too. I can see how pathetic I was before and he's made me so much stronger. I'm never going to just settle for someone. I got on with Ben so well and trusted him; but he ruined it and he's just going to go back to his fake life in Perth and have a baby with his girlfriend. That actually makes me pity him. How can you want to settle for that after this amazing experience? With that attitude he's definitely not the right man for me.

It's been a life-changing experience for everyone. Cara said that talking to Bailey – before she sucked him off – has made up her mind to go travelling. He told her about travelling around Australia and learning to surf on Bondi Beach and holding a koala bear at the Steve Irwin Zoo in Brisbane.

Cara: "Sure I can't go back to baking cakes in Dublin when I could be holding a koala in Australia. I'm gonna go home and save every penny I can."

Zoe's excited to live in LA to try and crack Hollywood. Good for her for giving it a go and not letting her dickhead 'friend' who runs the drama department drag her down. After gay Pete and Danielle go to Florida she's going to apply to be a teacher. Watching her get the kids to clean up the bunk was incredible. She'll be a great teacher, fun, but won't stand for any shit. Pete's just going to carry on being fabulous back at Manchester University.

Coming to camp has definitely made me feel more powerful and increased my confidence in myself and how I am around others. Thinking about all my new friends from South Africa, Australia, America and even Ireland now amazes me. I've mountain biked in the New York wilderness, taken a leap of faith and stayed semi sane looking after more than 35 kids, 24 hours a day, six days a week for the past three months. I'm proud of myself.

Tuesday 23rd August

12:19pm Oh my god, I am so hungover. I've got a pounding headache. About 50 of us counselors went around the lake last night for a warm up goodbye party. Think everyone's conveniently forgotten about the bears, including Danielle after she was so horrible to me the other day. I was having a right old chat with the second-session bitches round the lake. I don't know why Cara and me started calling them this; they're actually really sound. I hate it when I start making friends as it's coming to the end of something. I guess everyone is letting their guards down now and so it's easier to get to know each other.

Pete is so up himself. Last night he looked sad so I asked him what was wrong.
Pete: "I don't think I'll ever get a boyfriend. I've never met anyone nearly as fit as I am".
Wow.

Argh, there's this kid in the radio shack who chooses it every day – wish he'd just piss off so I can go to bed. He's been the only one to turn up lately and is super, super nerdy. He's got dorky glasses, a snotty dripping nose and although he looks like he'd know quantum physics, he's actually as thick as shit. Good chance to write my diary I guess. I need a poo.

My bunk kids are fucking me off to the max at the moment. Tegan and the super counselor just don't leave me alone. They always want to be near me and they tell me they love me all the time. It should be really sweet, but I just find it weird. Another one of my girls, the one who ripped the pages out the bible, Helen, is a little witch. Everything she says is some bitchy pointless comment then she'll say "only joking!" at the end as if that makes it ok. The one whose mum has cancer came with her best friend and I'm guessing this best friend is bored brainless with all the sadness in the bunk. She seems to see me as the only fun one and she's always getting in my face doing stupid expressions.

Annoying camper: "Lucy, quick Lucy, look."

I look up and she'll stick her face in mine with her tongue out and eyes crossed, or some similar twisted face, and it drives me crazy. It's gross. I just look forward to them all going – brats. Camp for me was all about the kids from the first session.

6:58pm Rebecca reckons they've asked her to be the Head of Music next year but she turned them down. There is *no way* that's true. All she does is play violin now and again in the pit. To be Head of Music at one of the biggest and best camps in America you'd need some serious skills and experience on your CV. Why does she lie so much?

Rebecca: "Yah, I would have loved to, they offered me all this money, but blah blah bullshit..."

Tinnitus, my arse.

7:39pm I'm laughing at my memory of DJing at canteen the other night. I sped up the BPM on the *Cha Cha Slide* song so all the kids were dancing like maniacs to keep up. It made me laugh, a lot.

Cara really likes Bailey now and she's upset that nothing more has happened between them. I think she would've liked a last-minute summer fling there. He seems all right, but I guess now that he's obviously told everyone what she did he's not going to want anything more serious with her. He probably thinks she's a right trash bag. Men's double fucking standards.

Wednesday 24th August

12:12pm Went for the last night out up at the GC last night. It was also one of the guys from visual arts' birthday. One of the other counselors had made him a cone bra to wear, with another cone for a hat – he looked like a right nobber, but seemed to like them. On the way home we 'borrowed' a golf cart again and went for a spin. Then we hung out in the dining hall till about three, just chatting and getting seriously stuck into some coco pops. Ben and me left everyone to it and went and said our first goodbyes down at the waterfront.

Ben: "I'm really sorry for not telling you I had a girlfriend back home."

Me: "It's ok, I'm over it now. It doesn't matter anymore anyway."

Ben: "I just wanted you to know I think you're amazing and if things were different we'd definitely be together."

It was sweet, but too little too late. I've already accepted that this relationship has a definite end – in three days in fact – so I'm not going to get upset when that end comes. We sat on the beach, had a bit of a kiss and lay down together, then just conked out. We managed to wake up before anyone saw us, thank god, and get back to our bunks.

11:34pm It's a cliché, but this summer has been an emotional rollercoaster. There have been a few occasions where I've never felt so free – coco pops fights, mountain biking, joyriding in golf carts, racing up the iceberg – but then times where I've felt totally and utterly trapped too. There's no way out of here. You can't leave by yourself, we're in the middle of nowhere and there's no bus to catch. If you don't finish the summer you lose any wages earned and you have to pay for your flight home. None of us students have the money for that. I've tried not to think about that – I'd go crazy with helplessness and claustrophobia. It's such a surreal world here with no TV, newspapers or radio. All that matters is what's happening here and now – it's a pretty cool way to live, for a while anyway. We've got three days left at camp, well most of us have. Some people are staying on another week to get camp packed up properly. From tomorrow we have to start taking down the decorations and putting stuff away in storage ready for next year. It feels really sad; I know time will go way too quickly, it already has.

Thursday 25th August

9:12am Cancun in three days! We booked accommodation in NYC as well, in some shithole of a hostel for the few days after Mexico and before our flights home. I'm so excited – I can't wait to lie on the beach all day and chill out. Rang mum earlier to tell her I was going and got told off for not phoning her enough over the summer. I'll see her in about two weeks though, looking forward to it.

7:19pm One of my campers – the one with the ripped bible – came up to my woodwork class today. I like it when the kids come and hang out with their dear old counselor it makes me feel loved. We sat chatting and sandpapering a piece of wood to make it look like we were doing something if Bud came around – although he rarely does. They don't care about us up at visual arts. She was asking all about Ben and whether we'll still be together after camp. I tried to get her off the subject, but it didn't really work. She was very sweet, saying how she really wanted a boyfriend as lovely as Ben. Awwww.

The guy I teach woodwork with is so chilled – he's one of the most laid-back people I've ever met. He seems fine with the fact I can't actually be trusted to make anything too. I have helped some kids with chairs and boxes and shelves, but I just like cutting stuff out on the jigsaw – well until I get lazy and put too much in and it spazzes out and the blade breaks, or I saw through their frame. He helped this kid to make a full-size dog kennel and the little boy is so proud of it, it warmed my heart. I hope he can take it home in the car though – it's massive.

10:17pm I saw the younger kids in *The Little Mermaid* tonight. It was so cute and one of the most popular plays on the schedule – people were stood up outside the theatre trying to watch because all the seats were full. I love that story and all the songs. I do think that I could have done a better job singing *Part of Your World* and lying on that rock though. I've been in practice for that part my whole life.

All the other counselors were really excited to meet this super famous actor off *Seinfeld* tonight – his kid's here and was in the show. Never seen it, so didn't even know who he was.

Friday 26th August – last day of the kids!

11:12am Oh god, incredibly embarrassing moment earlier. Yesterday Tegan told Zoe and me she was going to miss us so much so she wanted to give us something to remember her by.
Zoe: "$100 should do it."
I laughed and told her to shut up. Then today Tegan's mum presented us with a $100 note each. Nearly died of embarrassment when she gave it to us. But, hey ho, another $100 for Mexico!
12:23pm Aww, Keakuki came and found me out to give me a big hug earlier, which was nice. She was off and wanted to say bye.
Her: "You're my favourite counselor Lucy, I love you. See you next summer. You better come back!"

And then she ran off to get on the bus going to the airport. I guess it is a long way for her parents to come, all the way from Hawaii to get her, but I hope they give her lots of love when she gets home. Poor kid.

2:24pm Just had another very odd moment involving Tegan and her family. I had lunch with them all in the canteen, and her mum was telling me how Tegan's biological mum and dad split up, then her dad got with a woman, and her mum got with that woman's ex-husband. So now they're like some happy, weirdo, swinging foursome. Tegan smelling her brother's hat in a sexy way seems to make a bit more sense now. I hope I managed to act casual when they introduced themselves, each to their own.

I'm so much more confident with the kids' parents now; I just stroll up and introduce myself. It makes me laugh to think of myself cowering on a bunk when the girls from the first session arrived. I was shitting it! I don't know why I was so scared of them before. Not sure what I thought they were going to do to me.

5:44pm By about midday the last of the campers had left. I was sad to say bye for the fourth and final time, but I don't think I really connected with my campers as much as in the other sessions. When I think of session four, I'll always associate it with the kids being moany and sad all the time. It feels weird not to have to prepare for another round of kids this afternoon, that's it!

We had a goodbye meeting with Earl and Bud. They thanked us for the summer and said it had been 'emotional'. I guess for them 2005 will always be remembered as the summer of Anna,

Jamie and Leith. Looking around at the meeting you could see the exhaustion on everyone's faces – we're a shadow of our June-time selves. It was sad to say bye to Earl and Bud, unless I come back to camp I'll never see them again. I went and gave Bud a hug, but I was too scared to hug Earl. Would've been weird seeing as I've barely spoken to him all summer. We left the Kennedy Theatre for the final time and they played *Piano Man* over the loudspeaker – bought a tear to my eye. We got the rest of our money from the front office and they gave us all the same excellent reference. All that was left to do was gather up our stuff and prepare for the last night on camp.

Saying bye to Rebecca tomorrow is going to be weird. I'll be sad to say bye, but glad not to have to see her again. Maybe a bit of time and distance between us will improve things – I'm not saying that I'll never see her again, but I doubt it.

10:57pm I'm crying out on the bunk porch. I can't believe tomorrow will be the last time I ever see Ben, it's too much to think about. I'd been trying to be strong and not let myself get too worked up about it, but I can't. I don't want to cry in front of other people, especially as I've been putting on a hard exterior all this time and claiming that I haven't felt the same about him since I found out about his girlfriend. I'm just going to let it all out now and be fresh for the morning.

Saturday 27th August

9:10am Loudspeaker: "Eeeeeeeeeeeevvverybody up, up, up! It's time to riiiise and shiiine... It's a beautiful day on the Rockbear campus..."
It's made me want to rip the loudspeaker off the pylon outside our bunk all summer, but now I just want to cry. That was the last time I'll hear that.

11:15am So wow, last day at camp today! I'm so sad. I walked around the grounds and took it all in, taking loads of photos. We had our final breakfast – Pete was filling his bag with cheeses and breads to eat for the next two weeks as everyone's scared to have to start paying for food and drink again, all our money's gone on shit at Walmart. The same shit that is now impossible to fit in my

suitcase. I tried to get my jacket back off Pete.
Pete: "Oh god yeah. Oh it's all packed now, can I give it you back when we're in England?"
Fucking fucker.

11:14pm We got our bags from the bunks and boarded the coach to JFK airport. I sat next to Ben, although really I wanted to sit next to Cara. There's just too much between me and Ben to have anything to say to each other now – we know we're not going to see each other again, I don't want to and I don't want to pretend. We're not two people who would be together in the real world, but at the same time I've never felt closer to anyone. He knew things about me, what I felt and meant, without me even saying. He's the most significant guy that's ever been in my life, but I don't feel like I need him and life will definitely go on without him.

We chatted on the way and laughed together, but without really saying anything serious or about 'us'. When we got to the airport he had a hotel nearby for the night with his mate and asked Cara and me to go with him, but I don't think he really wanted us to or he would've asked before. I didn't want to go anyway. This was the end and I had my eye on Mexico. He thanked me for a brilliant summer and we had a kiss and a cuddle and that was it. That really was it! It was so weird and anti-climactic after all these weeks of dreading saying goodbye to him. Sometimes I wish I was more physically sensitive. I know other people were looking at me to cry – but I really just didn't feel like it. I'd let it all out last night and today I didn't even shed a tear.

I said bye to Pete and Danielle – they went off to get their flight to Florida. We promised we'd see each other again and I'm sure we will. I felt more happy that I'd made some friends for life rather than sad at leaving them. Rebecca just went! She didn't even find me to say bye. Wow, that's a sad end to 12 weeks of sharing a bunk and our lives.

I'm sleeping at the airport tonight with Cara, Pip and Emily. We've set Britney's pink duvet out on the floor and we're all bedding down for the night on that.

Sunday 28th August

10:18am Barely slept at all last night. Cara and me are waiting for our flight. I've got so much shit compared to her – three massive cases to be precise – she just chucked everything away that she didn't need, I've kept every single little thing.

I'm going to miss Pip and Emily so much. I can't believe I won't be seeing them all day every day anymore; it's such an odd feeling. Saying bye to Emily this morning was sad, she's been a great friend at camp, but she's going off to stay at one of her campers' houses in Chicago. I'll see her when we get back to Sheffield, for sure. We've both got another year there and we'll be living close to each other.

And Ben. I'm glad it ended like that. It was a perfect way to end a relationship really, a slow and mutual splitting up. It was a fun and sweet summer romance that I'll always remember. At times I felt so intensely about him, but others I really wasn't bothered at all.

Saying bye to everyone else was weird. Zoe and me just hugged and she made me promise to go see her if ever I'm in Australia. It's a shame her and me shared a bunk – we would have been friends if we didn't have to work together. I will look her up when I'm in Melbourne though. No one was really crying. We've all just had such a crazy and surreal summer, at times it felt like I wasn't actually in the moment. Like I was a bystander watching all this craziness going on and I might not actually be part of it. I mean, take today. I was in JFK Airport in New York City having just had the best summer of my life in a kids' summer camp up in the mountains. I'm saying a sad goodbye to some of the most incredible people I've ever met in my life from all over the world. This time last year I was working in a summer office job in the next town to where I grew up. Is this really my life? I hope so. It's absolutely amazing. And even though I'm completely worn out physically and mentally I can't wait to go back to camp next year. Although, at this second the exhaustion is saying never, ever again.

8:19pm Mexicoco!